El Greco

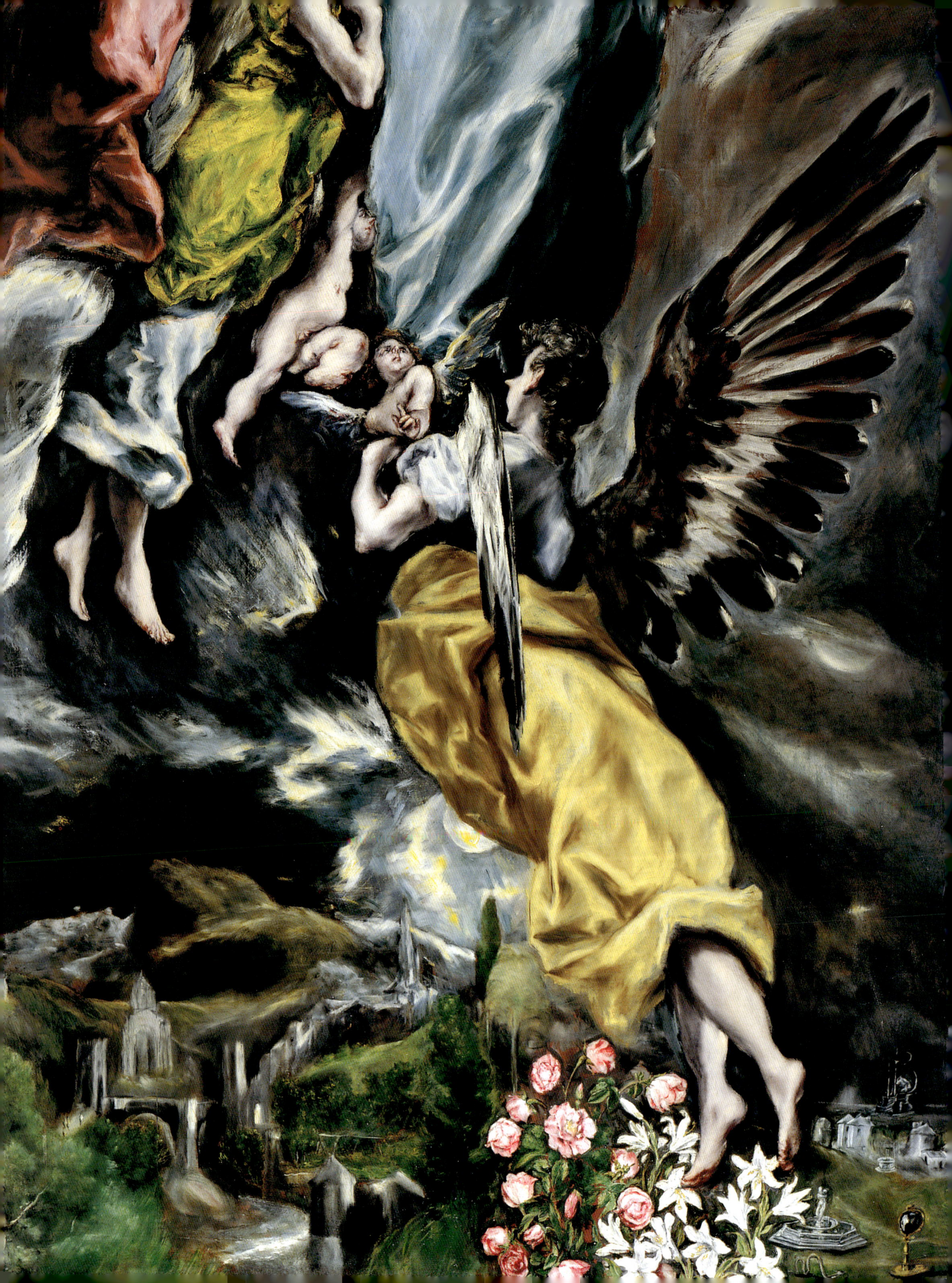

XAVIER BRAY

El Greco

CHRONOLOGY BY LOIS OLIVER

NATIONAL GALLERY COMPANY, LONDON

DISTRIBUTED BY YALE UNIVERSITY PRESS

GlaxoSmithKline is proud to be sponsoring *El Greco*, an unprecedented collection of work that shows the full scope and breadth of the achievement of this unique and distinctive artist.

El Greco is the latest in a series of landmark exhibitions that GSK has supported in recent years, which includes *American Sublime* and *William Blake* at Tate Britain, *Grinling Gibbons and the Art of Carving* at the V&A, and here at the National Gallery, *Spanish Still Life* and most recently, *Art in the Making: Underdrawings in Renaissance Paintings*. Our partnerships with Britain's galleries and museums are built on a shared commitment to excellence, innovation and access. We are also committed to supporting arts projects that involve the participation of young people from an early age. Through our support we hope to encourage new audiences and ask those already familiar with the arts to take a fresh look.

Themes of discovery and innovation are fundamental to a research-based company like GSK. With his uniquely recognisable style and dramatic use of light and colour, El Greco is, perhaps, one of the most distinctive and recognisable artists of all time. However, after a long period of neglect after his death, he was rediscovered by painters of the late nineteenth and early twentieth centuries, including Manet and Picasso. This exhibition shows the full range of El Greco's subjects and the development of his style and artistic ideas; it includes not only his most famous pieces but also some of his less well-known work, including portraiture, landscapes and sculpture. We hope that you will leave the collection having rediscovered El Greco, with a greater understanding of the breadth of his artistic achievement, imaginative power and visual sophistication.

Please enjoy the exhibition.

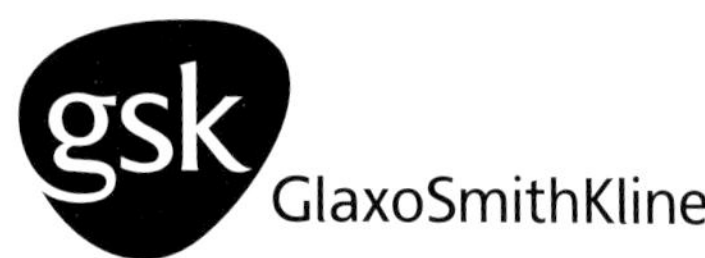

Since his rediscovery by artists and critics in the nineteenth century, El Greco has been perceived by many as the most 'modern' of the Old Masters. His work played a central role in the development of twentieth-century art. Paul Cézanne, Franz Marc and Jackson Pollock all studied and admired his paintings. His bright and powerful colours, his elongated forms and ecstatic expressions continue to startle and provoke us today. Indeed, he is often seen as an artist working outside his time – a proto-modern, misunderstood in his own day and waiting to be rediscovered.

Such an approach, however, is misleading, as this book sets out to show. Xavier Bray explains how El Greco came to paint in such a 'modern' style and tells the fascinating story of a painter who, in the late sixteenth century, left his native island of Crete in order to cross half of Europe in search of new artistic horizons.

Published to accompany the London showing of the exhibition *El Greco*, organised jointly by the National Gallery and the Metropolitan Museum of Art, New York, this book is designed to provide the reader with an outline of El Greco's odyssey from producer of small-scale icons in Crete to creator of giant altar paintings for churches in Toledo, Spain. Countering his reputation with some as an eccentric painter thought to have suffered from astigmatism, it presents him instead as a deeply thoughtful artist searching for a visual language through which to express contemporary religious thought.

El Greco's achievement was to transform the mysteries of religion into graspable visual representations. He modernised the idiom of the post-Byzantine icon into large and colourful compositions of mystical visions that made his works appear modern in his time and continue to do so today.

The National Gallery would like to thank GlaxoSmithKline for so generously sponsoring the exhibition in London and for assisting us in presenting El Greco to a contemporary audience.

Charles Saumarez Smith
Director, The National Gallery, London

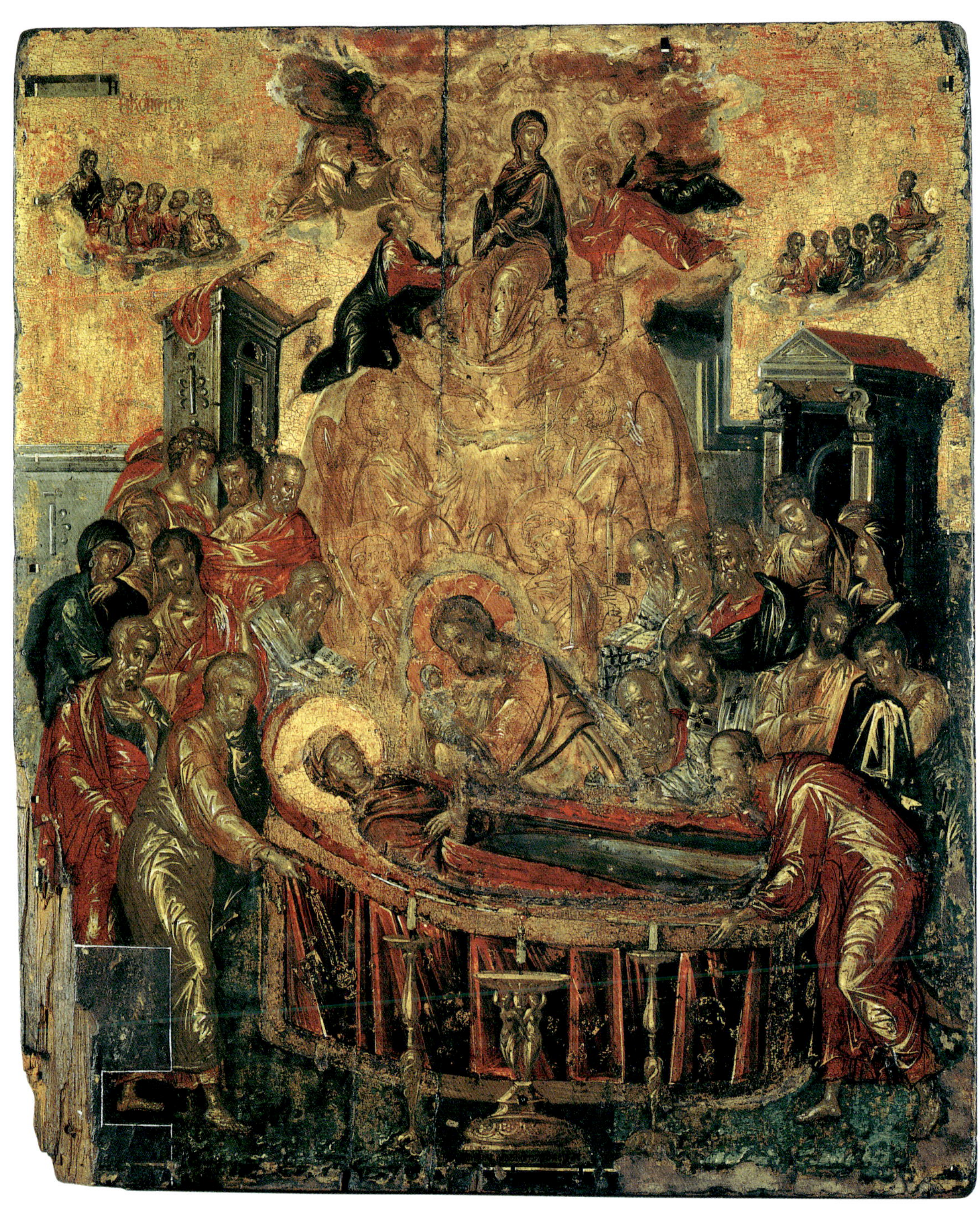

1. *The Dormition of the Virgin,* before 1567

Tempera and gold on panel, 61.4 x 45 cm
Holy Cathedral of the Dormition of the Virgin, Ermoupolis, Syros

The Greek of Toledo

For many people, the name El Greco conjures up visions of brightly coloured paintings dominated by strangely proportioned figures with elongated bodies. Why did he paint in such a peculiar way? And who would have wanted to purchase such bizarre compositions? Was El Greco a mystic who translated his visions into paint? Did he suffer from a problem with his eyesight, perhaps astigmatism, as an ophthalmologist once suggested? Or was he a rebel seeking artistic emancipation and trying to break as many academic rules as he could? When the National Gallery bought El Greco's studio version of *The Agony in the Garden of Gethsemane* in 1919, it caused a public outcry. The Gallery's then director was accused of buying a painting by an artist who not only could not paint but was also deranged. Although the art critic Roger Fry defended El Greco's manner of painting – comparing him to Cézanne and admiring his 'purposeful distortion and pulling of planes' – the painter's work was largely misunderstood by the general public.

In fact, the great quantity of paintings produced and sold by El Greco during his thirty-seven years in the Spanish city of Toledo suggests that none of the theories cited above is correct. On the contrary, commercial records show that El Greco enjoyed a successful career as one of the most esteemed artists of his time. He rented palatial rooms in the heart of Toledo and is said to have had musicians play while he supped. He enjoyed philosophical debate and wrote treatises on painting, sculpture and architecture. He owned an extensive library and was bequeathed books by his scholarly friends. His workshop churned out versions of his paintings for sale in Madrid and Seville, as well as Toledo. With his son, Jorge Manuel (1578–1631), he ran the early seventeenth-century equivalent of an interior decoration firm, supplying paintings, altarpieces and sculptures for ecclesiastical clients.

El Greco's ability to assimilate different artistic techniques and approaches to religion and philosophy led him to develop one of the most original styles of painting in the history of European art. However, for nearly three hundred years following his death in 1614, the artist was derided, misunderstood or simply forgotten. Not until nineteenth-century intellectuals and artists recognised El Greco's genius did he once again become a focus of aesthetic appreciation. These new

admirers, from Delacroix to Degas and Picasso, knew little about
El Greco's life or thinking. His early works were still unknown, and they
could judge him merely on the pictures that he painted in Spain. Only
in 1983, when cleaning revealed El Greco's signature on an icon of *The
Dormition of the Virgin,* in a church on the Greek island of Syros, was
there full evidence to prove that he began his career as an icon painter,
working in the tradition-bound post-Byzantine school of painting (fig. 1).

Born Domenikos Theotokopoulos on the island of Crete, El Greco
remained loyal to his Cretan roots throughout his life. He was a
conscientious member of the Greek communities of the cities where he
lived, Venice, Rome and Toledo, and on several occasions he provided
financial aid to Greeks forced into exile by Ottoman invaders. He even
acted as an interpreter in 1582 at nine court hearings for a seventeen-
year-old Athenian servant accused of heresy by the Spanish Inquisition.
The fact that he signed his works in Greek throughout his career
demonstrates how strongly he felt about his Greek identity.

However, it was perhaps the difficulty of pronouncing his name
that led his contemporaries in Italy and Spain to call him El Greco (the
Greek). He was born in 1541 in Candia, a bustling port and the capital of
Crete, known today as Iraklion. His father, Giorgios Theotokopoulos,
was a tax collector with shipping and trading interests and the artist's
elder brother, Manoussos, followed in their father's footsteps.

Strategically placed in the Mediterranean midway between the
Western powers of Christendom and the Islamic Ottoman empire, Crete
was at that time an important trading centre. Although the island had
been a Venetian colony since 1211, its Greek Orthodox inhabitants
continued to look towards Constantinople as the centre of their religious
world until the collapse of the Byzantine empire in 1453, when the city
fell to Islamic invaders. Thereafter, Crete became an important centre
for the Orthodox Church, as clerics and scholars sought refuge on the
island. By the sixteenth-century, Catholic Venetians and Orthodox
Greeks were living together in relative harmony, with intermarriage at
all levels of society bringing the two communities closer. Greek families
sent their children to universities on the Italian mainland and the
Venetian ruling elite assimilated Greek customs. Both cultures were
united against a common enemy, the Ottoman Turks, who eventually
conquered the island in 1669.

El Greco's family was almost certainly Greek Orthodox, but the
relaxed policies of the island's Venetian rulers made for a climate of
religious tolerance. Catholics and Orthodox attended each other's

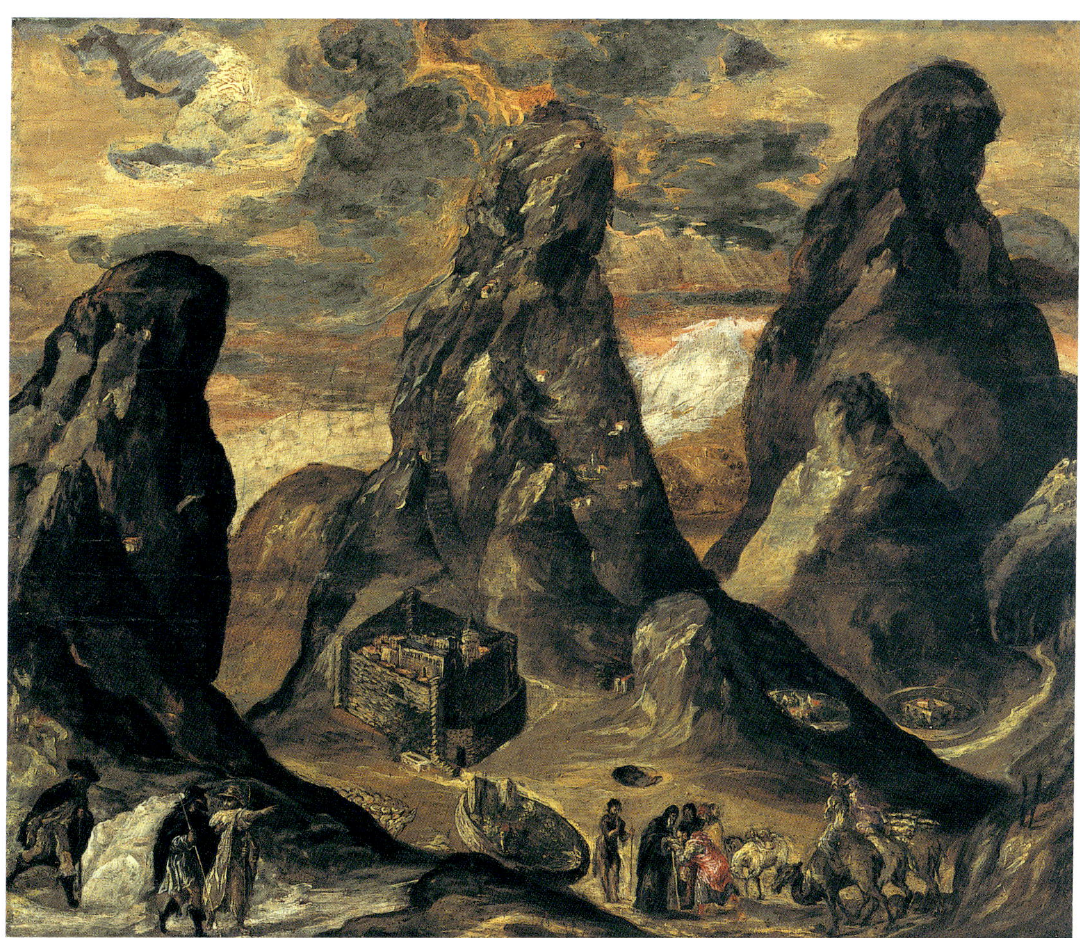

churches and joined together in the religious ceremonies and
processions that marked the annual calendar of Candia. In this
environment, El Greco would have been able to familiarise himself with
both Orthodox and Catholic forms of worship and their accompanying
theologies. Among the many churches and convents of Candia were two
major religious centres: a large Franciscan convent on the edge of the
town (containing works by Venetian artists such as Giovanni Bellini)
and the Monastery of Saint Catherine, a place of Orthodox culture and
learning in the heart of the city. As a painter of icons, El Greco may have
discussed artistic and theological issues with both the Orthodox monks
and the Franciscan friars.

A painting by El Greco that illustrates the Orthodox culture so
fundamental to his work is *Mount Sinai* (fig. 2). Painted on a small
wooden panel, it shows a series of craggy peaks. In the middle,
shrouded in clouds is Mount Horeb – where Moses received the tablets
of the Ten Commandments from God. To the right is Saint Catherine's
Mount, where the early Christian martyr was buried, while at the foot

of Mount Horeb a walled complex represents the monastery dedicated to the saint. It was the mother house of the monastery in Candia and contained a vast library and an enormous collection of icons.

We know little about El Greco's early career, but we may assume that he trained as an apprentice in one of the many workshops in Candia that practised the Byzantine art of icon painting. Rather than representing natural phenomena as perceived by the senses, icons were designed to give a glimpse into the transcendental world of their subjects. Figures were typically two-dimensional, elongated and uniform in size and proportions, while colours were saturated and brilliant with more of a symbolic than a descriptive function. Traditional practice, based on repetition, left little room for experiment or for personal development. In Crete, a flourishing trade in sacred images for the home market and for export had led to the development of a distinctive school of icon painting, in which Byzantine traditions were modified by western influences brought to the island by Venetian prints and paintings. By 1563, according to a document dated that year, El Greco was a master painter of icons with his own workshop.

That El Greco welcomed outside influences as a way of helping to make his images more visually compelling is demonstrated in *Saint Luke painting the Virgin and Child* (fig. 3). El Greco may have painted this icon as an examination piece in order to become a member of the Guild of Painters in Candia. As the patron saint of artists, Saint Luke would have provided a fitting subject. El Greco shows the evangelist in the act of painting the famous icon of the *Virgin Hodegetria*, patron and protector of Constantinople. The icon rests on an easel, below which is a stool with a box of pigments, a small circular vessel and a tablet. Seated on an elegant chair, Saint Luke holds a small palette and a fine brush with which he applies the last touches to the icon. The painting is badly damaged and the saint's face is no longer visible, but we can see how El Greco has subtly introduced perspective into his composition, adding objects such as a paint box to create a sense of realism and borrowing the pose of his angel from an Italian print. This combination of elements shows his eagerness to explore new means of expression.

On 26 December 1566, El Greco obtained authorisation to sell by lottery a painting representing a scene from the Passion of Christ, executed on a gold background and valued by two fellow painters at the relatively high price of seventy ducats. The money that he raised may have been intended to finance his travels, as the next record we have of the artist, from 18 August 1568, shows he is in Venice supplying a

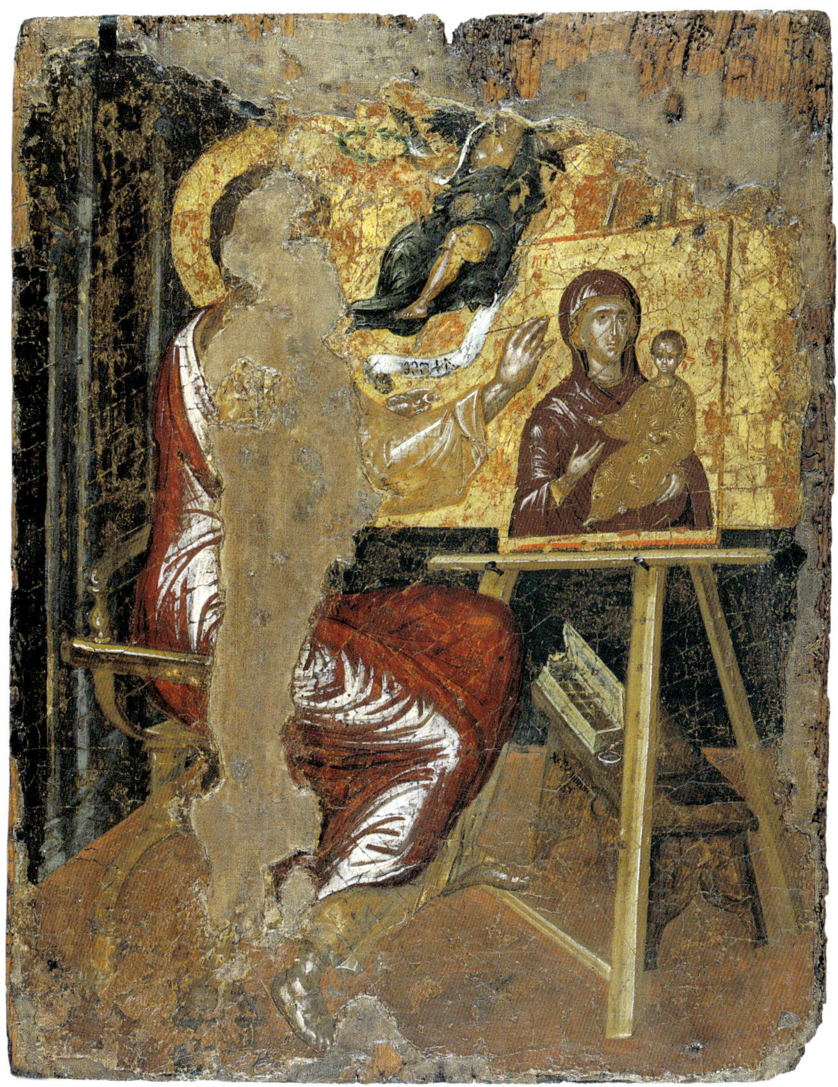

Cretan cartographer with drawings. Little is known of El Greco's stay in
the city, but he would have been able to study the works of Titian,
Tintoretto and Bassano in the city's churches and palaces. He may have
got to know the artists themselves, visiting their studios and observing
the respect with which they were treated by their contemporaries.

The transformation of El Greco's painting style during his time in
Venice is demonstrated in his first version of a subject that he was to
treat several times throughout his career, *The Purification of the Temple*
(fig. 4). Putting aside his Byzantine training, he experiments with
perspective and architectural backdrops. His figures are shown in
graceful and natural poses, while his colours become descriptive and his
treatment of light becomes more elaborate. The painting illustrates a
growing interest in architecture that was to pay dividends when he later

came to design the frames for altarpieces in Toledo. Among the books in his library, an annotated copy of Daniele Barbaro's edition of Vitruvius's *On Architecture* (Venice 1556) may have been bought in Venice at this time.

Despite the attractions of Venice, El Greco did not stay there long. The main centre for the arts in Italy was the papal city of Rome. In a letter dated 16 November 1570, the Croatian miniaturist Giulio Clovio (1498–1578) wrote to his patron, Cardinal Alessandro Farnese (1520–1589), telling him that 'a young Candiot, disciple of Titian', had recently arrived in Rome and was in need of lodging. In his letter, Clovio praised a now-lost self portrait by El Greco, which had apparently made a great impression on painters in Rome and asked whether the painter could stay in the cardinal's palace. Farnese agreed and El Greco not only obtained access to one of the finest art collections in Rome, but also a valuable entrée to a group of cultivated antiquarians, artists and churchmen.

Soon afterwards, in a portrait of *Giulio Clovio* (fig. 5), El Greco found an opportunity to show off the skills and techniques that he had learnt in Venice. Using the Venetian portrait format, he shows his subject standing by a window through which a landscape can be seen. While Clovio's head and hands are highly finished, the landscape and the book that he is holding are executed with broader, looser brushstrokes in a manner indebted to the late works of Titian and Jacopo Bassano. The volume to which Clovio points is his most famous work, the *Farnese Hours* (now in the Pierpont Morgan Library, New York), an illustrated text for devotional contemplation commissioned by Alessandro Farnese and completed in 1546. According to Vasari, Clovio in his old age took great delight in showing visitors this masterpiece, which had taken him nine years to produce and was known as one of the 'marvels of Rome'.

Little is known about El Greco's activity in Rome. He was registered as a painter at the Guild of San Luca in September 1572 and is known to have employed an assistant called Lattanzio Bonastri da Lucignano, possibly with a view to setting up a workshop and pursuing a career in the papal city. With the exception of a full-length portrait of *Vincenzo Anastagi* (The Frick Collection, New York), however, he does not seem to have received any major commissions. Instead, his artistic production was mainly confined to modest-sized pictures for private patrons, commissioned perhaps as a result of introductions from his friend Clovio.

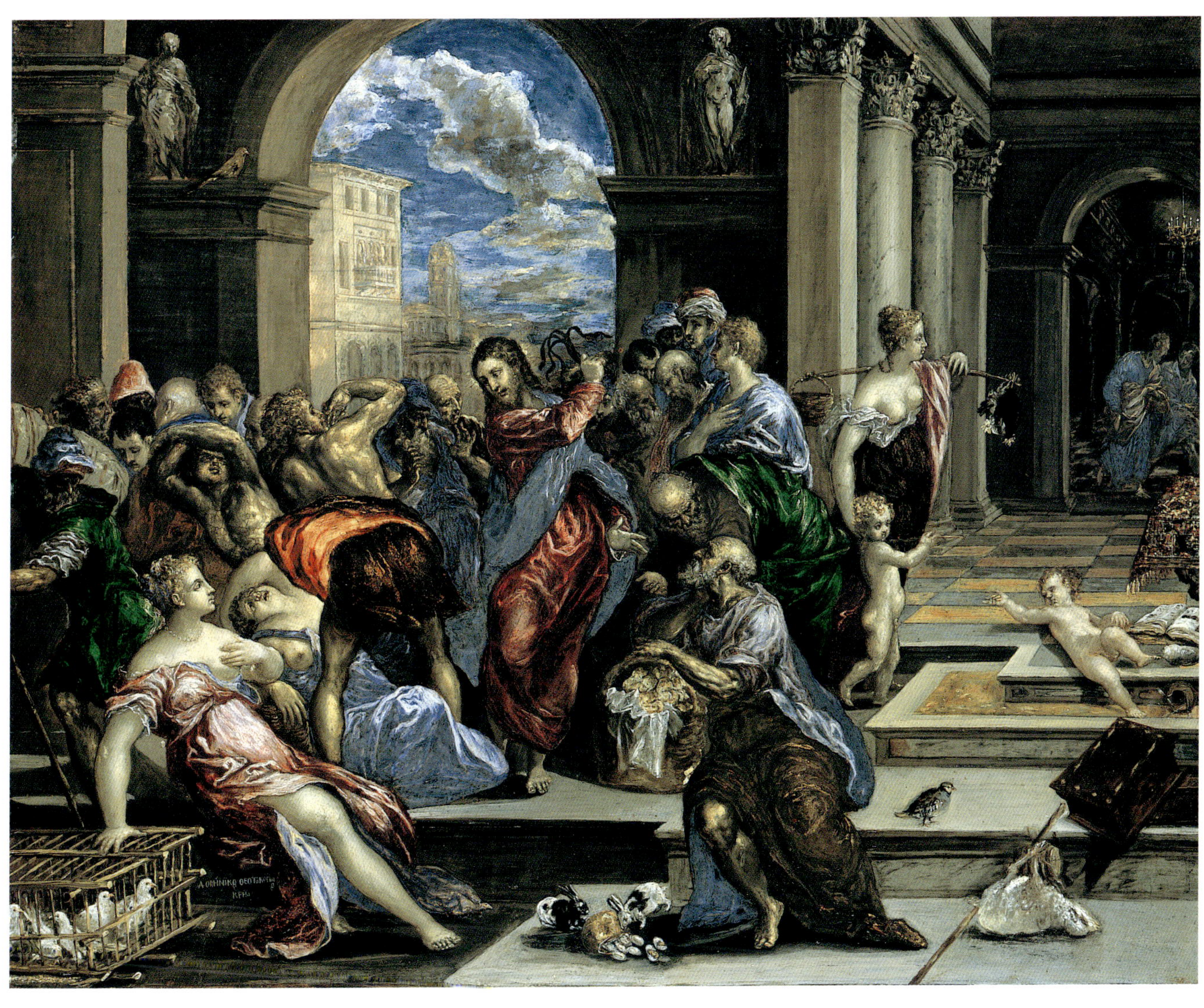

4. *The Purification of the Temple,* about 1570–1

Oil on poplar, 65.4 x 83.2 cm
National Gallery of Art, Washington, DC
Samuel H. Kress Collection
inv. 1957.14.4 (1482)

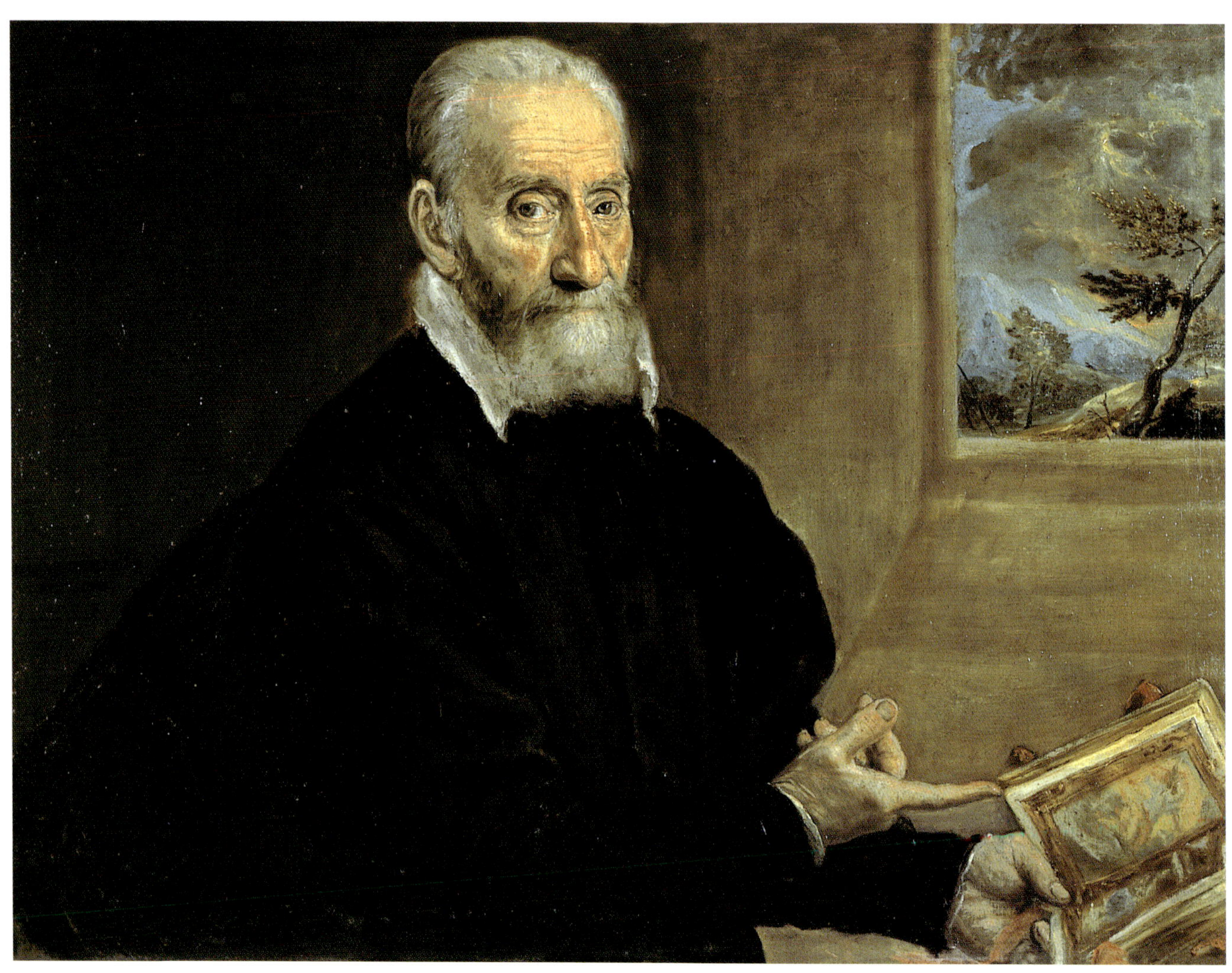

El Greco's knowledge of Greek and Latin would have eased his acceptance into the Farnese circle. Along with Clovio, he forged another important friendship with the cardinal's librarian, Fulvio Orsini (1529–1600), a renowned humanist, classical scholar and art collector who owned a large collection of drawings by Michelangelo. During El Greco's stay in Rome, Orsini acquired seven paintings by him, including *Mount Sinai* and a painting of *A Boy blowing on an Ember to light a Candle* (fig. 6). This *tour de force* of naturalistic representation

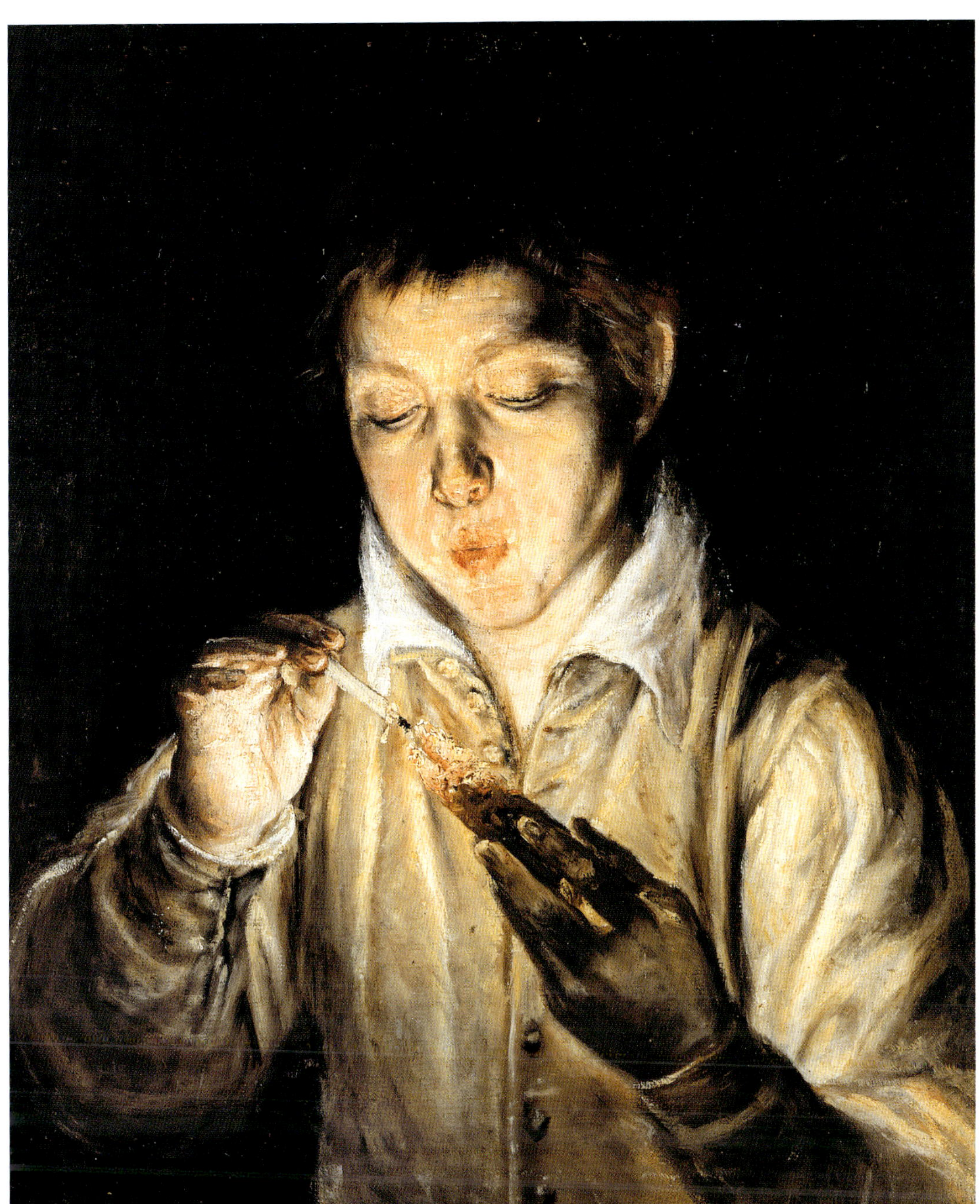

6. *A Boy blowing on an Ember to light a Candle ('Soplón')*
early 1570s

Oil on canvas,
60.5 x 50.5 cm
Museo Nazionale di
Capodimonte, Naples
inv. Q192

may have been inspired by a conversation with Orsini on the subject of classical art. Writing in the first century AD, the Latin author Pliny the Elder describes a painting of this subject by the ancient Greek artist Antiphilus of Alexandria, and El Greco's Greek roots and artistic ambitions may have prompted him to emulate this lost work.

One of the strongest influences on El Greco's work at this time was Michelangelo, to whose work he was probably introduced by Clovio. Writing in the margins of his own copy of Vasari's *Lives of the Artists*

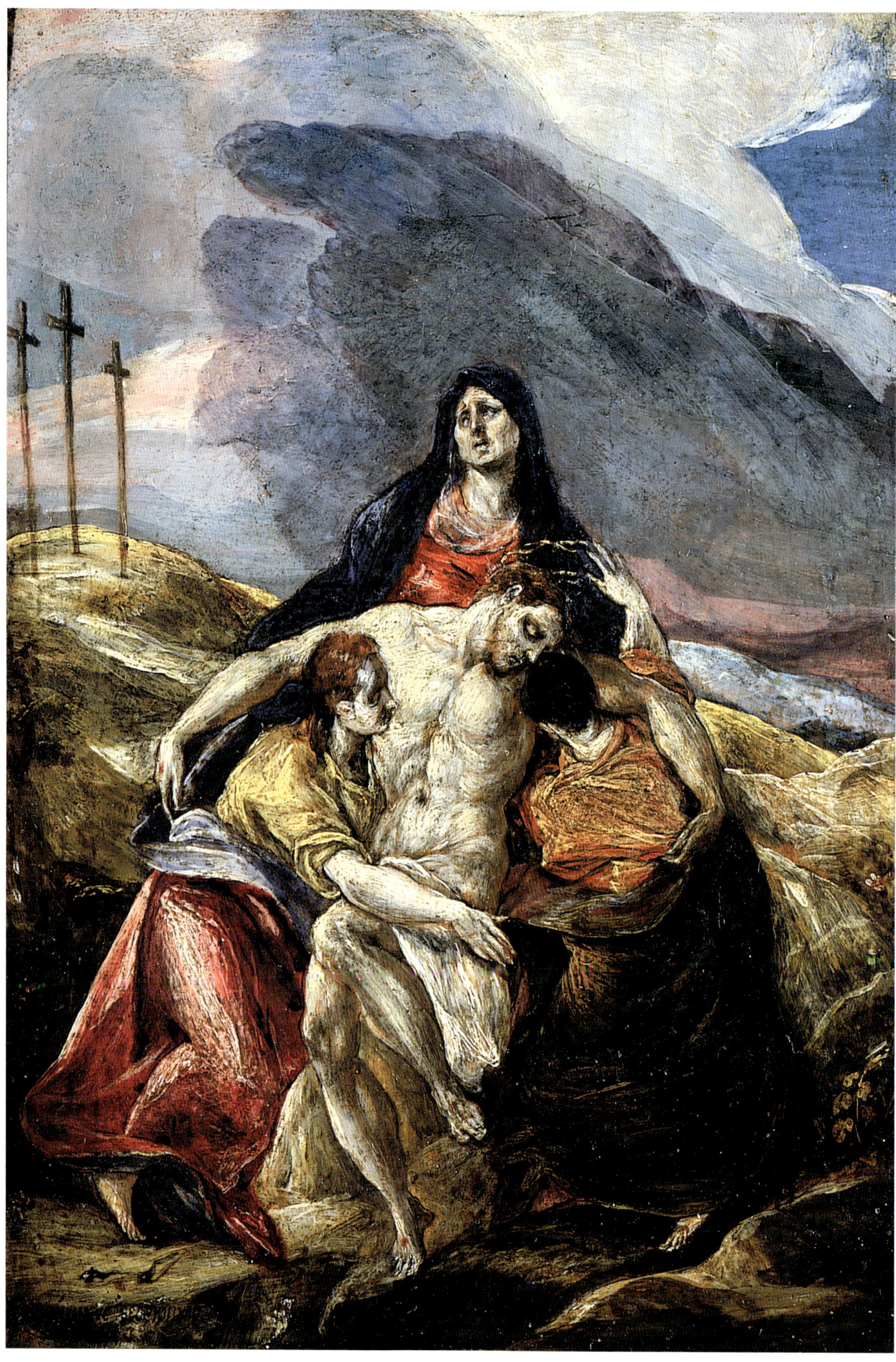

(1568), El Greco commented critically on Michelangelo's use of colour but praised his treatment of the human body: 'This is what he knew how to do best, and he did it better than anyone.' While Michelangelo's drawings gave El Greco ideas for some of his compositions, such as *The Purification of the Temple,* his sculptures also had a great impact, as is illustrated by a small painting on panel of the *Pietà* (fig. 7). El Greco had probably seen Michelangelo's sculpture (fig. 8), then in the Bandini collection in Rome, of the Virgin and Mary Magdalene holding the body of the dead Christ, with the standing figure of Joseph of Arimathea behind. El Greco borrows Michelangelo's pyramidal arrangement, focusing on the graceful heaviness of Christ's corpse. Mary Magdalene and Saint John support his outstretched arms while the Virgin provides the pinnacle of the composition as she looks heavenwards in distress. To enhance the emotional impact of his *Pietà,* El Greco draws on his Byzantine training, simplifying the drapery and applying several layers of paint to build up volume.

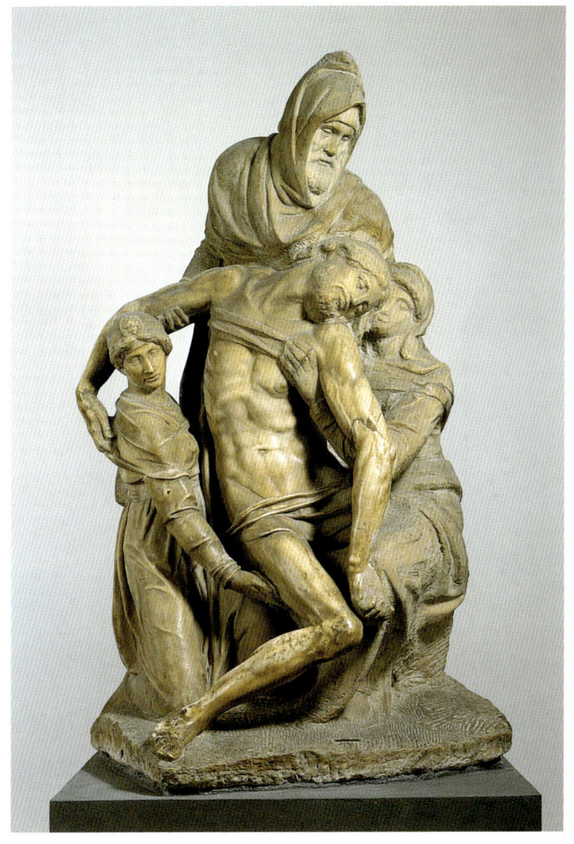

8. Michelangelo
Buonarroti, 1475–1564
Pietà, about 1550

Marble,
height 226 cm
Museo dell'Opera del
Duomo, Florence

El Greco's stay under Cardinal Farnese's roof terminated a year and half after his arrival in circumstances that remain unclear. El Greco no doubt thought highly of himself and if we are to believe the physician and amateur art historian Giulio Mancini (1568–1630), he was later forced to flee Rome for declaring that he was prepared to replace Michelangelo's *Last Judgment* with something more decorous. That may be an exaggeration, and it seems more probable that his departure was motivated, once again, by an ambition to seek new challenges. Whatever the case, on 21 October 1576, El Greco's name is recorded in a register of supplicants requesting financial assistance from the Royal Almoner in Madrid. Far from the bustle of the Roman art scene, it was in Spain that the artist was to develop the extremely personal style that marks him out today.

At the time, King Philip II of Spain was looking for painters to decorate his monastery-palace at El Escorial, outside Madrid. El Greco's

7. *Pietà,* early 1570s?

Oil on wood,
28.9 x 20 cm
The Philadelphia
Museum of Art,
The John G.
Johnson Collection

17

ability to communicate a religious message in pictorial terms may well have caught the attention of the librarian of El Escorial, Benito Arias Montano, who was a frequent visitor at the Palazzo Farnese. One of El Greco's first commissions in Spain was for a painting on canvas showing *The Adoration of the Name of Jesus* (Monasterio de San Lorenzo de El Escorial). The subject celebrated the victory in October 1571 of the combined fleets of Philip II, the Doge of Venice and Pope Pius V over the Ottoman Turks in Greek waters at Lepanto.

The genesis of the sketch on panel (fig. 9) for this painting is debated. While it may have been a copy after the painting in El Escorial, it is possible that El Greco had brought it with him from Rome as a demonstration piece. In it, the three allies, Philip II, the Doge and the Pope, are shown kneeling on a carpet with courtiers and crowds behind, worshipping the trigram of the Name of Jesus, *IHS*, which appears in a burst of glory at the top of the composition. The young man with a sword on the left may be Philip's illegitimate half-brother, Don John of Austria, who led the allied forces against the Ottoman Turks. To the right, the jaws of hell swallow the damned, while in the distance other people are being pushed by devils across a bridge into purgatory. Like other devotional paintings by the artist while in Rome, the back of the panel is painted in a *trompe l'œil* technique to emulate wood grain, as if to turn a simple panel into a decorative item fit for presentation to a client. The technique of decorating the back of a panel was very common in icons produced at the Monastery of Saint Catherine, Mount Sinai.

His treatment of this theme demonstrates El Greco's ability to transform a historical event into an image of religious propaganda. In it, he returns to the Byzantine tradition of breaking down realistic space in order to include multiple levels of interpretation in which politics and religion are intertwined. His association with Philip II was not to last long, however. That the two had very different approaches to religious painting is evident from the outcome of the only other commission that El Greco was to receive from the king, in around 1579. This was for a large altarpiece for a side chapel in the church at El Escorial, showing *The Martyrdom of Saint Maurice* (fig. 10). Completed in 1582, the painting was rejected by Philip, who almost immediately ordered a replacement to be made by the Italian artist Rómulo Cincinnato.

It is likely that El Greco had irritated the king by trying to be too clever in his treatment of saintly martyrdom. Instead of representing a bloody massacre in the foreground, as most other painters of the period would have done, El Greco chose to combine early Christian history with

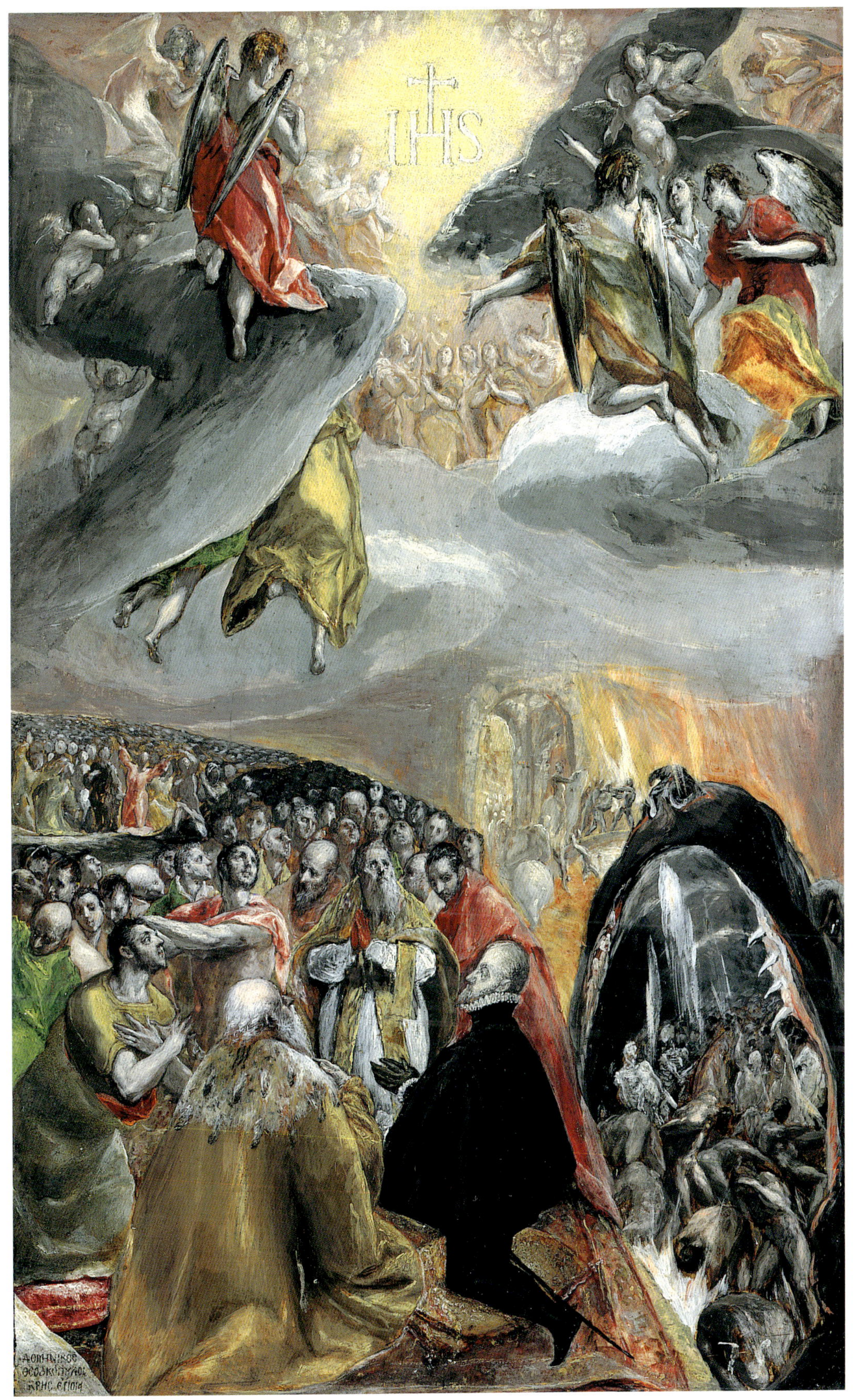

9. *The Adoration of the Name of Jesus*
late 1570s

Oil and tempera on pine, 57.8 x 34.2 cm The National Gallery, London, inv. NG 6260

contemporary history. Saint Maurice, the leader of an Egyptian legion of the Roman army and the patron saint of infantrymen, is shown discussing with his colleagues the merits of martyrdom: what it means for the Christian faith rather than sacrifice to pagan gods. In the foreground, El Greco inserted contemporary portraits of Philip II's generals, relegating the scene of the actual martyrdom to the background. Philip II probably regarded the presence of sixteenth-century generals in a painting of a third-century martyrdom as inappropriate, and El Greco's intellectual rendition of the theme would have been far removed from the king's taste for realism in such matters.

If royal patronage was not to be forthcoming, there were other options for El Greco. To the west of Madrid, Spain's ecclesiastical capital, Toledo, offered opportunities for a skilled painter capable of satisfying a sophisticated intellectual audience, and it was there that El Greco turned, in the summer of 1577, to offer his services as a painter of religious ideas. Diego de Castilla (1507–1584), who was the dean of Toledo Cathedral and father of Luis de Castilla (one of the Spanish ecclesiastics whom El Greco had probably met in Rome), quickly provided him with two commissions. The first, signed on 2 July, was for a painting for Toledo Cathedral, and the second, on 8 August, for nine paintings for a funerary chapel that Diego de Castilla had recently built alongside the Cistercian convent of Santo Domingo el Antiguo.

The painting for the cathedral took as its subject the Disrobing of Christ before his Crucifixion (fig. 11). It was originally destined for an altar in the vestiary, where the priests put on their vestments to celebrate Mass. In a dynamic treatment of his subject, El Greco shows soldiers and common people crowding around Christ and glaring at him while he looks up to heaven, preparing for his coming sacrifice. In the lower part of the painting, the Virgin Mary, Mary Magdalene and Mary Salome contemplate the cross, at the base of which a man is making a hole for the nail that will impale Christ's feet. The crowded, almost claustrophobic composition is adapted from Byzantine icons and the red carmine of Christ's garment symbolises his coming Passion.

Nothing like this had ever before been painted in Spain, and the cathedral canons, unaccustomed to such a powerful composition, disapproved. They refused to pay his asking price of 900 ducats, complaining that the three Maries had no place in this scene as they were not described as being present in the Gospels and that it was improper for El Greco to have placed the heads of people in the crowd above the head of Christ. The dispute was the first of many that El

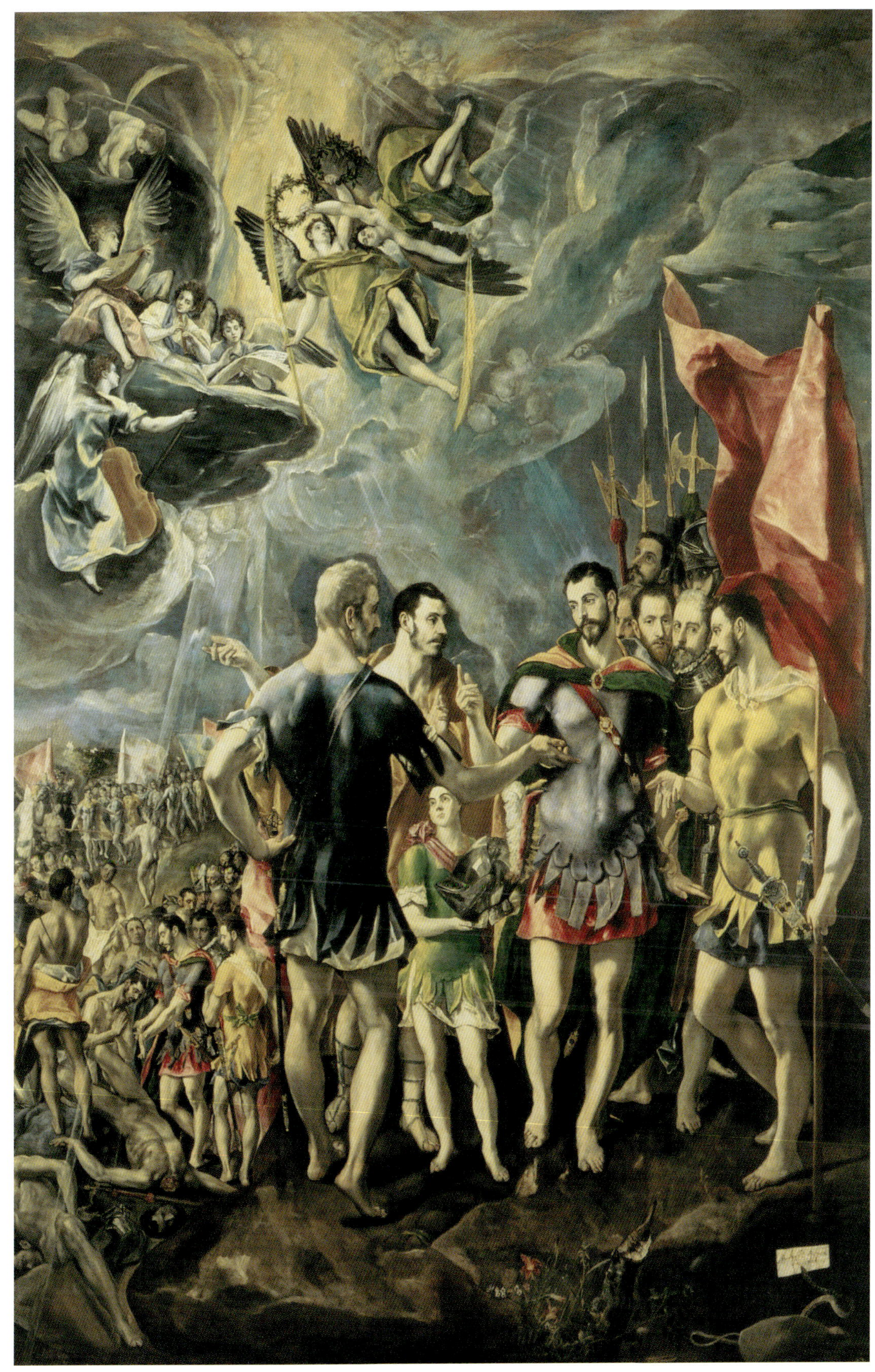

10. *The Martyrdom of
Saint Maurice*, 1580–2

Oil on canvas,
448 x 301 cm
Monasterio de San
Lorenzo de El Escorial,
Patrimonio Nacional

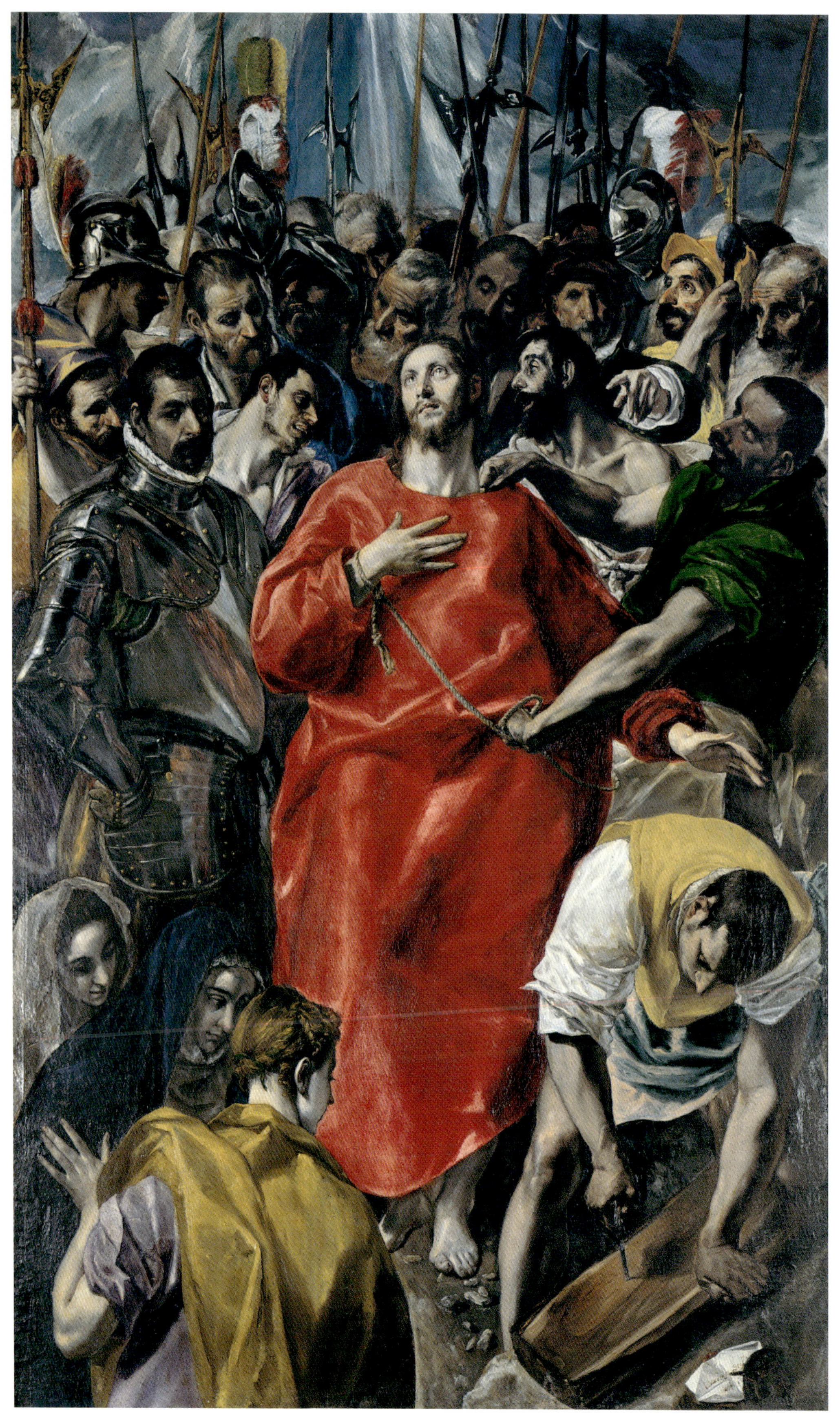

11. *The Disrobing of
Christ ('El Espolio')*
1577–9

Oil on canvas,
285 x 173 cm
Sacristy, Toledo Cathedral

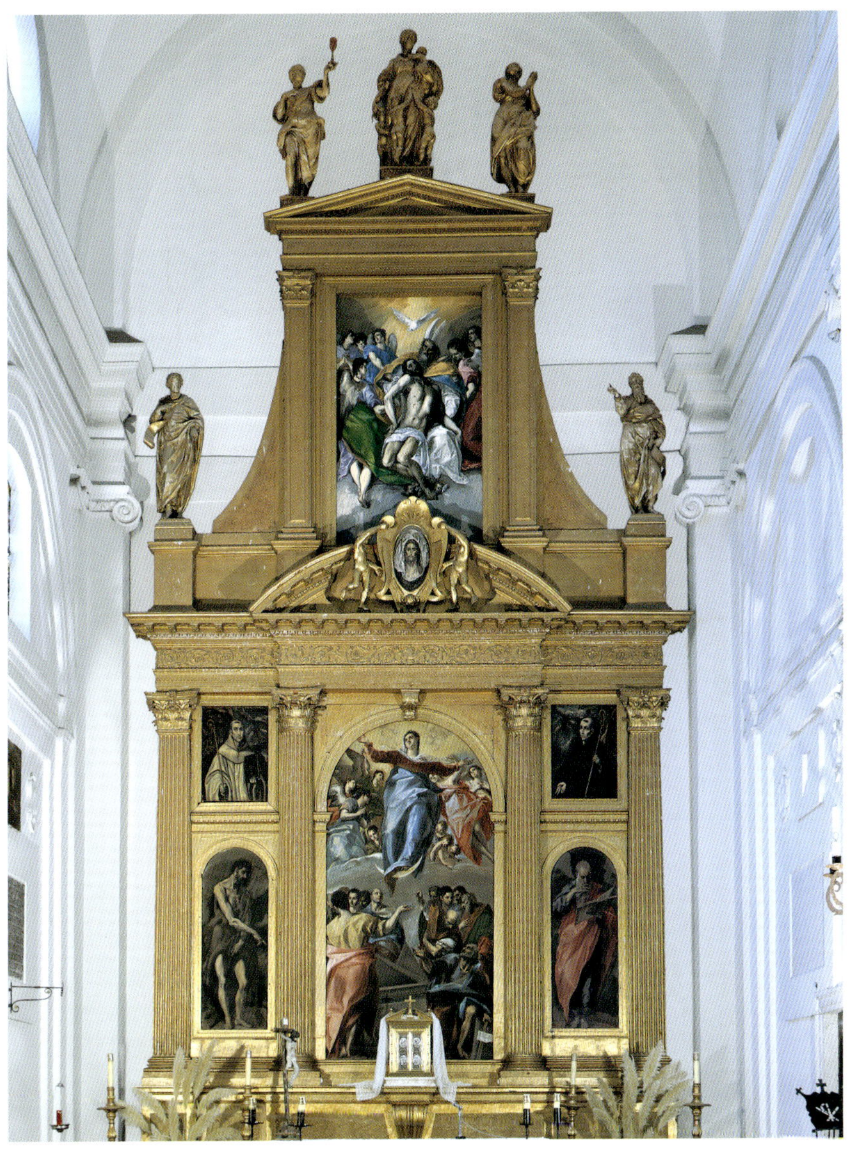

12. High Altar of the Church of Santo Domingo el Antiguo, Toledo

Greco was to find himself embroiled in with his clients in Spain. After lengthy argument, he finally settled, on 8 December 1581, for the much lower price of 350 ducats.

The second commission from Diego de Castilla was to become one of El Greco's finest achievements. In addition to producing nine paintings El Greco took responsibility for the whole ensemble, putting into practice all that he had learnt in Italy about designing altar frames and the sculptures adorning them. The two side altars showed the *Adoration of the Shepherds* and the *Resurrection*, while the main altarpiece (fig. 12) contained seven works including the *Assumption of the Virgin* and the *Trinity* (both these works were replaced with copies when the originals were sold in the nineteenth century, they are now in the Art Institute, Chicago and the Museo del Prado, Madrid respectively).

This ambitious project was funded by a bequest from Doña María de Silva, a Portuguese noblewoman who had entered the Cistercian convent after her husband's death in 1537 and remained there until her own death in 1575. Although she never took the vows of a nun, she wore the habit and demonstrated exemplary piety. As the executor of her will, Diego de Castilla was responsible for ensuring that she was fittingly buried. Diego was reputed to have been her lover and he stipulated that he wished to be buried alongside her, with his illegitimate son, Luis, whose mother was rumoured to have been Doña María.

The iconography of the altarpiece, with paintings of the Infancy of Christ, his death and Resurrection and the Assumption of the Virgin, relates to the themes of mortality and redemption. In the centre, the Virgin Mary, the mother of Christ and the epitome of feminine virtue, is being taken up to heaven, defying mortality. Above her, the body of Christ is held by God the Father. The strong vertical lines of El Greco's design, both architecturally and pictorially, lead the eye of the viewer to ascend into heaven. Some years later, El Greco was to choose this chapel as the location for his own tomb.

Whilst working on these paintings El Greco settled in Toledo, sharing a house with Jéronima de las Cuevas, who is thought to have featured as a model in many of his paintings and who in 1578 bore him a son, Jorge Manuel. They never married – indicating perhaps that El Greco had already been married when he left Crete – although this did not prevent the artist from entertaining good relations with the many clerics, lawyers, university professors and merchants who made up Toledo's establishment. Aided by Francesco Prevoste, the assistant who had accompanied him from Rome, El Greco was able to provide them with art works in tune with their religious convictions and spiritual aspirations.

Among the commissions that he received in these early years in Toledo, one from his parish priest, Andrés Núñez de Madrid, for the church of Santo Tomé exemplifies what attracted contemporaries to El Greco's work. This large canvas shows *The Burial of the Count of Orgaz* (fig. 13), a fourteenth-century nobleman known for his generosity in funding local religious institutions such as the Augustinian convent of Saint Stephen. According to the legend, Saint Augustine and Saint Stephen appeared miraculously at the count's funeral at his parish church of Santo Tomé, lowering him into his tomb themselves.

In his representation of the event, El Greco included portraits of living people among the crowd, with Nuñez de Madrid himself as the

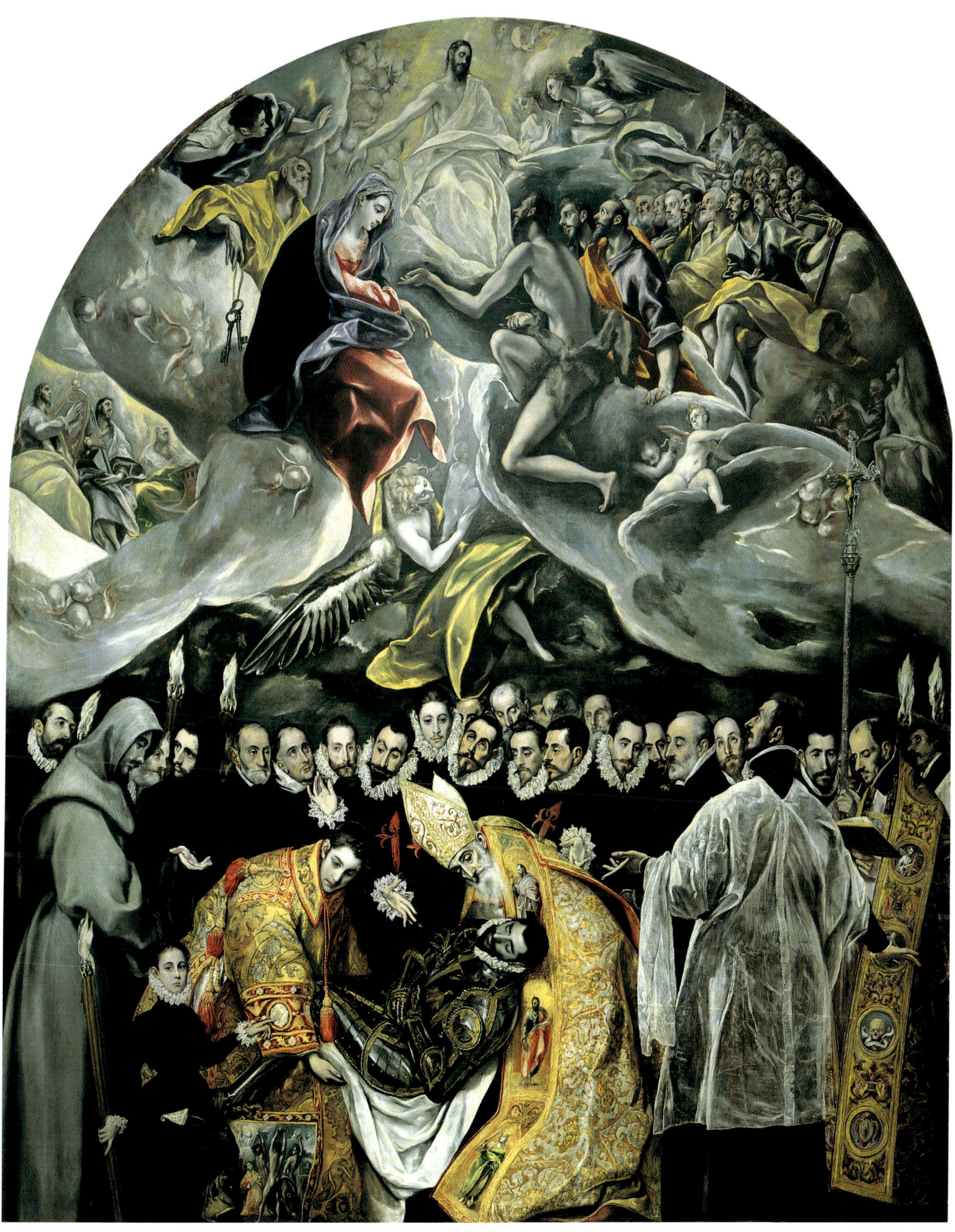

priest officiating at the funeral. Other figures are thought to include
El Greco's friend, the antiquarian Antonio de Covarrubias, with a white
beard, and his own son, Jorge Manuel, then around eight years old,
shown pointing at the miraculous apparition. Above the crowd, in a
sudden change of register, El Greco shows the mystical world of the
afterlife, in which an angel carries the soul of Orgaz – in the form of
a baby – through a cloud to the Virgin and Saint John the Baptist,
intercessors with Christ in recognition of his good works. Saint Peter
stands ready with his keys to heaven, while on the other side Philip II,
in the company of the Apostles and Saints, witnesses this glorified
entrance to the next world. The colours are bright and filled with light,
while the figures are elongated and vary in size according to their
hierarchical position in heaven. The whole makes up a highly effective
visionary representation of a heavenly apparition.

For those who understood El Greco's sophisticated theological
allusions, he was a perfect choice of painter to fly the flag of religious
renewal and reform in the face of the threats to Catholicism posed by
the Ottoman empire in the East and the Protestants in northern Europe.
The Council of Trent, meeting between 1545 and 1563, had imposed
Catholic doctrine to counter the rising influence of the Protestants.
Artists such as El Greco were enlisted into the campaign as visual
interpreters of the spiritual messages that the Catholic Church and its
supporters wanted to put forward. In Spain, the process of religious
affirmation, in the wake of the fall of the Islamic kingdom of Granada
in 1492, coincided with a sharpening of pressures on the country's
Moorish and Jewish inhabitants to convert to Catholicism. In Toledo,
where a blend of Moorish, Jewish and Christian cultures had produced
a rich artistic and literary heritage, a growing number of Catholic
hardliners were pressing for religious conformism and racial purity.
In 1547, the then Archbishop of Toledo had passed a statute of *'limpieza
de sangre'*, or purity of blood, excluding from ecclesiastical office and
benefices anyone with a trace of Jewish lineage over four generations.
Toledo's role was to provide spiritual support for the military and
political campaigns of Philip II, an ardent defender of the Catholic faith.

El Greco's paintings portray the city itself in that light. His *View of
Toledo* (fig. 14) is not a topographical vista of the town and its architectural features, but a vision of an ideal city, a new Jerusalem. The spire of
the cathedral has been deliberately moved towards the centre of the
composition to emphasise the presence of the Church. The imposing
Alcázar, or royal residence, has been moved to the left, standing out

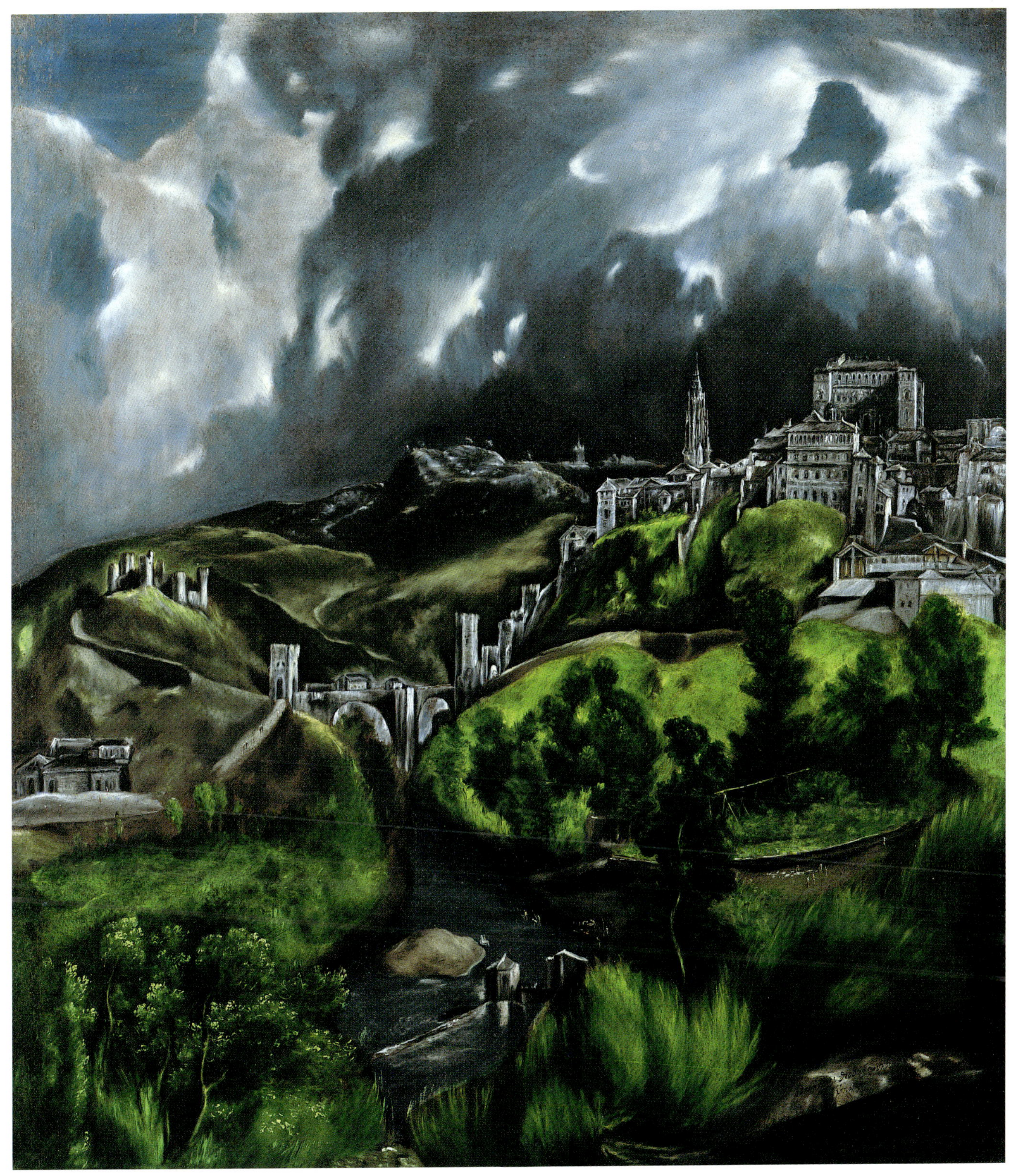

14. *A View of Toledo,* about 1597–9

Oil on canvas, 121.3 x 108.6 cm
The Metropolitan Museum of Art, New York
H.O. Havemeyer Collection, Bequest of Mrs H.O. Havemeyer, 1929, inv. 29.100.6

against the other buildings and embodying the State as the supporter of Religion. Above this earthly scene, light bursts through the heavy clouds indicating the proximity of heaven and the spiritual world. A version of this painting is thought to have belonged to El Greco's friend and admirer, Pedro Salazar de Mendoza (about 1550–1629), an ecclesiastical scholar and administrator of the Tavera Hospital, which El Greco was later to decorate. Mendoza had a great interest in Toledan history and owned several maps and views of the city, which he maintained had been a centre of faith and civilisation from the earliest days of the Church's presence in Spain. In terms of 'orthodoxy, customs, laws, courtesy, urbanity and good language,' he claimed, Toledo was unsurpassed in the world.

Like Mendoza, El Greco's other patrons were mostly open-minded ecclesiastics infused with a spirit of Christian humanism, rather than hardliners in the mould of the Spanish Inquisition. The Archbishop of Toledo appointed in the year of El Greco's arrival in the city, Gaspar de Quiroga (1512–1594), pursued a policy that reflected the best ideals of Tridentine Catholicism. Others among El Greco's supporters and admirers included university professors and theologians interested in the writings of the early church fathers such as Saint Augustine and their relevance to the contemporary Church, but open, also, to the classical philosophy of Aristotle and Plato in accordance with Toledo's tradition of cross-cultural exchange.

El Greco's ability to provide decorative schemes with a strongly propagandistic Catholic message is visible in a commission that he received on 9 November 1597 from a friend, Dr Martín Ramírez de Zayas (1561–1625), professor of theology at Toledo University. The professor's late uncle, Martín Ramírez (1499–1569), had been a rich merchant of Jewish extraction and a devotee of Saint Teresa of Ávila. Inspired by Saint Teresa's devotion for Saint Joseph, Ramírez left money in his will for the construction of a chapel in his honour (fig. 15). It was Zayas's responsibility to ensure the completion of the chapel, and to decorate it he ordered four paintings from El Greco. The main altarpiece was to depict a *Saint Joseph and the Infant Christ* with a view of Toledo as the backdrop, and above it a *Coronation of the Virgin*, both still *in situ*. For the side altarpieces, Zayas commissioned *Saint Martin and the Beggar* (fig. 16) and *The Virgin and Child with Saints Martina and Agnes*. While part of the purpose of these paintings was to demonstrate Martín Ramírez's conversion to Catholicism, thereby justifying his interment in a Christian chapel, they also served to illustrate his charitable activities

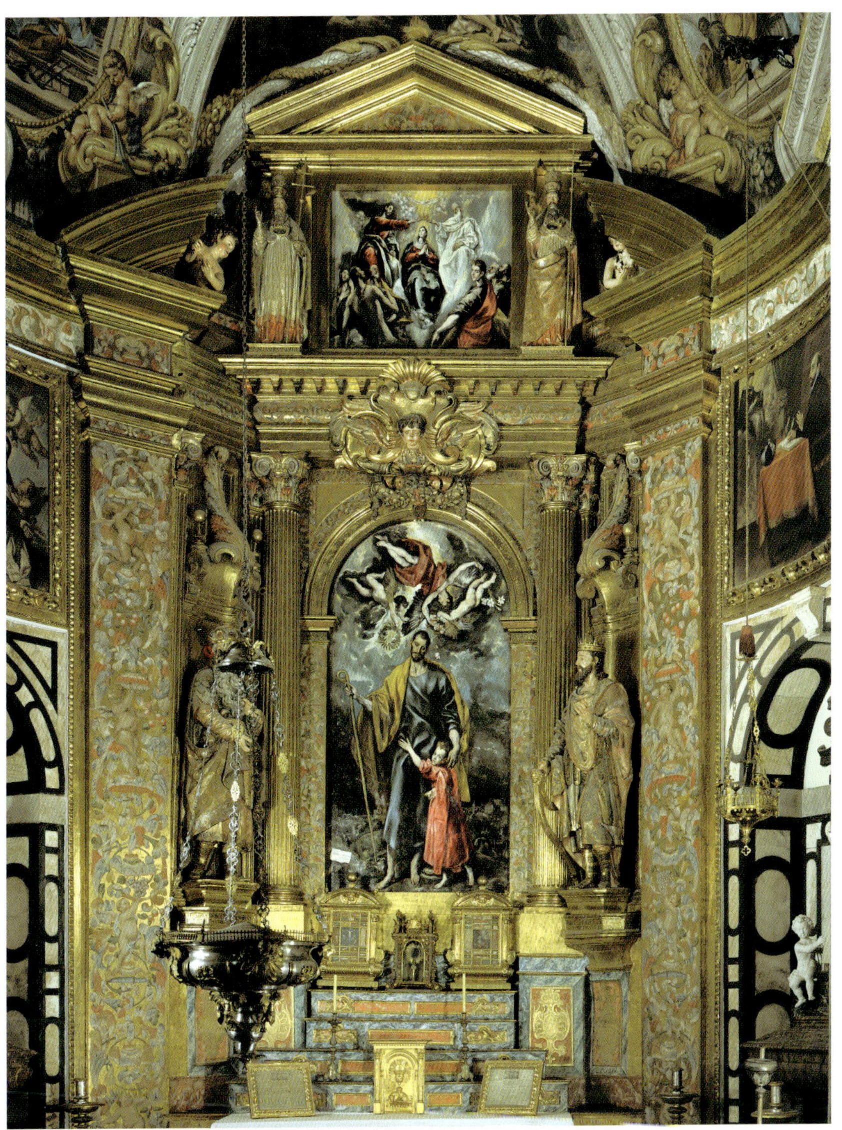

during his lifetime. Saint Martin, Ramírez's patron saint, is shown in
the act of cutting his cloak in order to give one half to a beggar. To
situate the saint's charitable act in a contemporary setting, El Greco
depicts him in a damascened suit of armour similar to those made in
Toledo at the time, set against a view of the city.

El Greco's ability to transmit a spiritual message through the visual
medium of paint on canvas or panel was fundamental for his clients.
As Mendoza wrote, 'paintings provide very powerful persuasion, greater
than that which is taken from writing, as long as they accord with
tradition and historical accounts. Because painting stirs and elevates the
spirit more than writing. The reason, as Saint Augustine explained, is
that ... what we know from writing, we know, as though by hearsay,
and this is worth less than painting, which puts it before the eyes.'

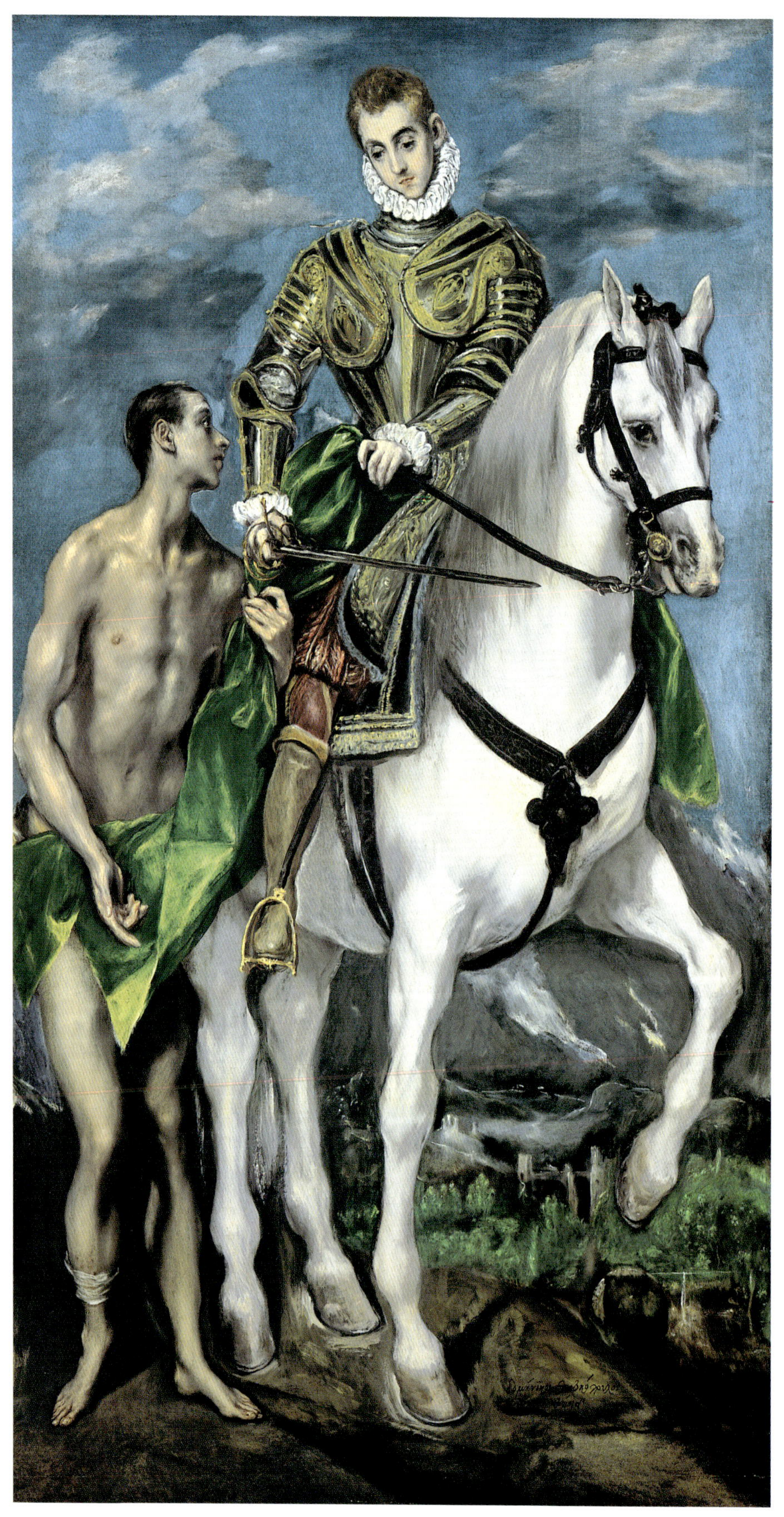

16. *Saint Martin and the Beggar,* 1597–9

Oil on canvas, with a
wooden strip added at
the bottom,
193 x 103 cm
National Gallery of Art,
Washington, DC
Widener Collection
inv. 1942.9.25

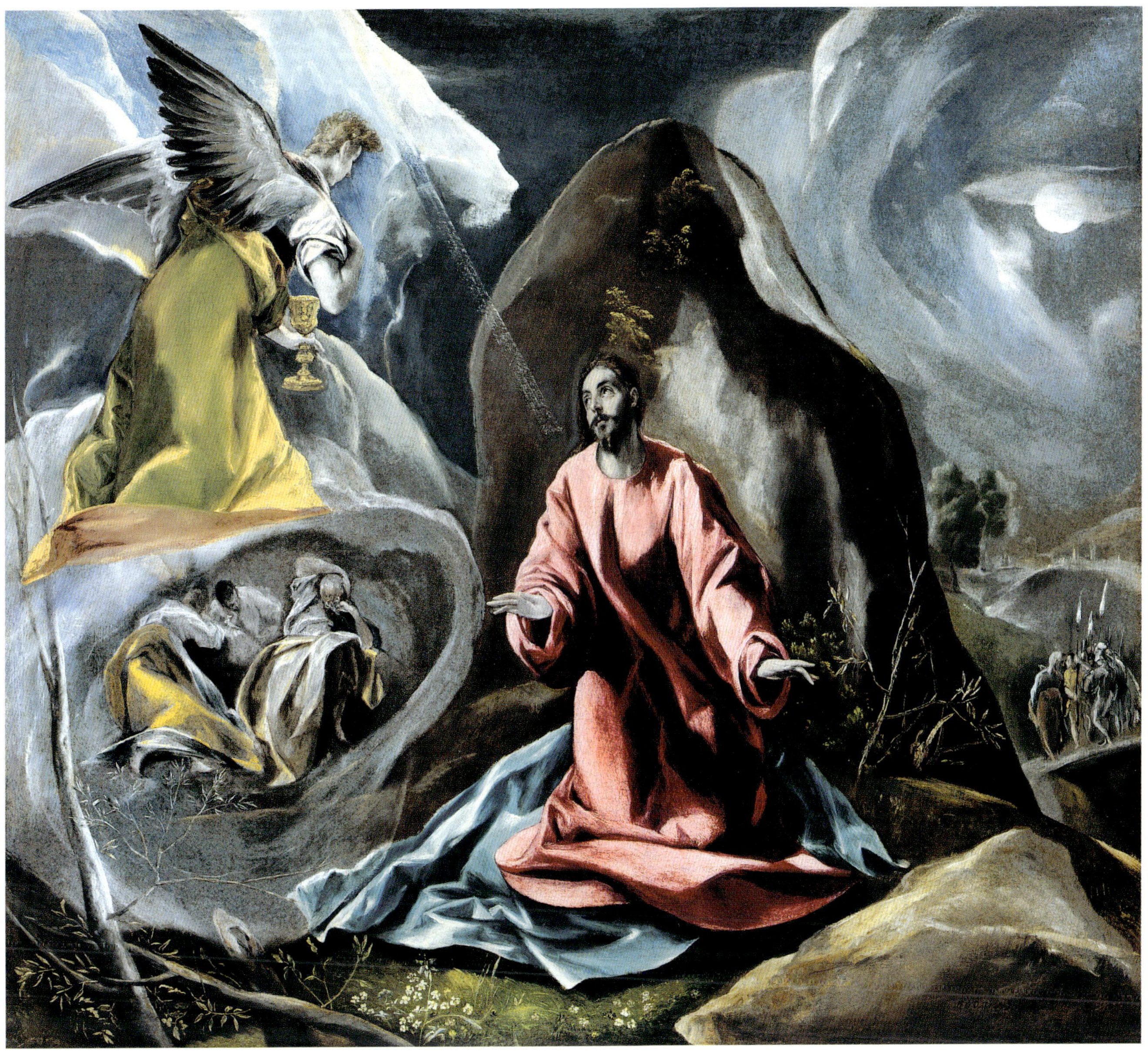

This visual immediacy was fundamental, too, for the transmission of
the spiritual teachings of Saint Teresa and Saint John of the Cross, who
inspired many of the members of the Toledan intellectual class with
whom El Greco was in contact. The writings of these mystics called for
the liberation of the soul from the constraints of the physical world, and
for direct communication with God. In *The Agony in the Garden* (fig. 17),
painted in the early 1590s, El Greco shows Christ in deep meditation as
he faces an angel who presents him with a chalice – the vessel in which
the wine of the Eucharist is lifted up by the priest during Mass –
symbolising his forthcoming sacrifice on the Cross (Matthew 26:39).
Nearby, three of Christ's disciples lie asleep, while in another part of the

17. *The Agony in the
Garden,* early 1590s

Oil on canvas,
102.2 x 113.7 cm
The Toledo Museum
of Art, Toledo, Ohio
Purchased with funds
from the Libbey
Endowment,
Gift of Edward
Drummond Libbey
inv. 1946.5

painting a group of armed men are seen on their way to arrest Jesus. Amid the darkness, El Greco's colours glow with fiery intensity, the yellow of the angel's drapery clashing against the sacrificial red of Christ's robe, while the light of the moon shining through the clouds adds to the visionary drama of the scene.

The ecclesiastical politics of Toledo were far from simple, as Quiroga's predecessor as archbishop from 1558 to 1576, Bartolomé Carranza, had learned to his cost. Despite warning the citizens of Toledo of the dangers of heresy and immorality, Carranza fell victim to the Inquisition and was imprisoned for seventeen years. Mendoza and many others among El Greco's friends were supporters of Carranza, and the artist's painting of *Laocoön* (fig. 18), executed around 1610 and which he may have kept in his studio, has been interpreted as being an allusion to Carranza's travails. In Virgil's *Aeneid*, Laocoön was the Trojan priest who warned his people that the wooden horse left by their Greek besiegers outside the city's walls was an act of treachery. As he and his sons were preparing to sacrifice a bull at the altar of Neptune, they were strangled by sea serpents sent by the goddess Minerva. El Greco interprets the story with compositional dynamism and pictorial virtuosity, basing his contorted and foreshortened figures on examples of classical sculpture that he would have seen in Italy. He sets the scene outside the city walls of Toledo, with the wooden horse standing next to the Bisagra Gate, one of the principal entrances to the city, thereby linking the story with his adoptive home town.

In another example of the type of commission that he received from his reformist patrons in Toledo, El Greco reworked a theme that he had already treated several times in Italy, that of *The Purification of the Temple* (fig. 19). Now, however, he focused on the spiritual meaning of the subject, setting aside the rules of perspective and proportion that characterise his earlier versions painted in Italy (see fig. 4). The National Gallery picture, probably painted around 1600, is executed with tremendous energy. Christ drives the merchants from the Temple in Jerusalem, telling them: 'Take these things hence; make not my Father's house an house of merchandise' (John 2:16). Compared to his earlier version in the National Gallery of Art, Washington, El Greco has edited down his composition so as to make it as direct as possible.

In the middle, Christ whips a merchant on his right out of his way, the sweeping movement causing those around the man to stagger, fall or run away. Into the wall above this group, El Greco has inserted a relief of the Expulsion of Adam and Eve from the Garden of Eden, a

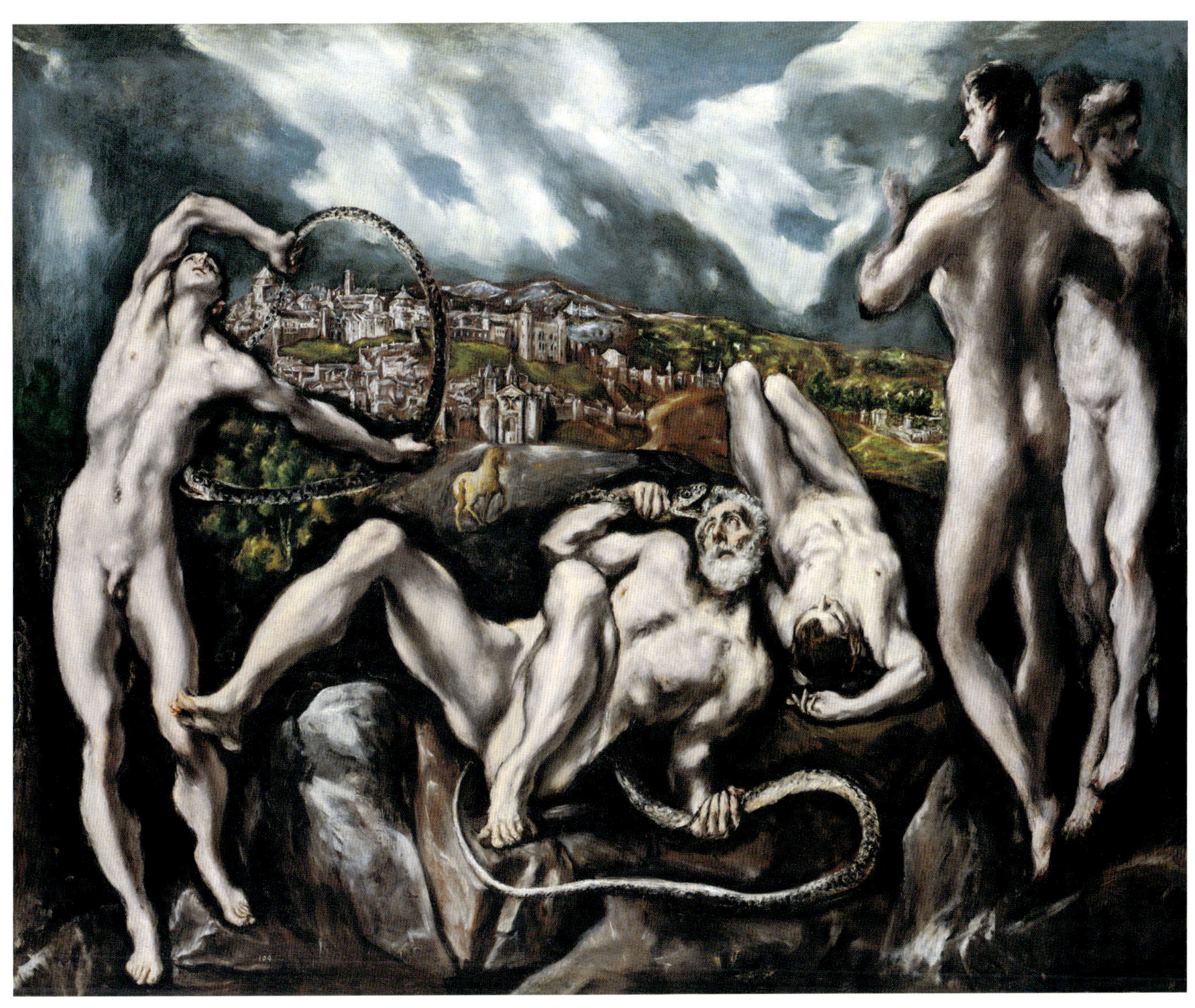

18. *Laocoön,* early 1610s

Oil on canvas, 137.5 x 172.5 cm
National Gallery of Art, Washington, DC
Samuel H. Kress Collection, inv. 1946.18.1

parallel to the action going on below. On the right, the group of Jesus' disciples conversing between themselves recalls Raphael's Vatican Palace fresco of the *School of Athens*, admired by El Greco. The relief above them shows the Sacrifice of Isaac, a prefiguration of God's sacrifice of his own son for the redemption of mankind. A young woman shown walking away from the scene may be the poor widow observed by Christ and his disciples putting two small coins in the Temple treasury, an act of generosity that Jesus contrasted with the painless largesse of the rich. This complex iconography can be read on many levels. The act of purifying the temple would have been seen by El Greco's contemporaries as an allegory of their efforts to cleanse the Church of commerce and hypocrisy. It may also have been seen as an exhortation to spiritual purity, likening the Temple to the soul that Christ cleanses from sin.

El Greco frequently had to fight to obtain the respect that he felt his art deserved, and even on occasion to obtain payment for works that he had supplied to clients. One such case was the Illescas affair, which resulted from a contract that he and his son signed on 18 June 1603 to decorate an altar dedicated to the miraculous image of the Virgin of Charity belonging to the Hospital de la Caridad in the town of Illescas, midway between Toledo and Madrid. When he came to claim payment for his painting of *The Madonna of Charity* (Hospital de la Caridad, Illescas), the hospital authorities objected to his inclusion of portraits of contemporary figures wearing large ruffs, including one said to be his son Jorge Manuel, and refused to pay El Greco's asking price. A lawsuit between the two sides was only resolved four years later, after it had gone from the archbishop's council in Toledo to the royal chancellery in Valladolid and to the papal nuncio in Madrid.

While El Greco was finally forced to accept a lower sum than he originally demanded, he nonetheless won a moral victory in successfully refusing to pay tax on the transaction, on the grounds that he was a practitioner of a liberal art and not a craftsman. This was the first time that an artist had received exemption from taxation in Spain, and the incident was subsequently cited by the painter Vicente Carducho (about 1570–1638), in his *Diálogos de la Pintura* (1629), in support of the thesis that painting was a liberal art. At around the same time as the Illescas affair, El Greco painted a portrait of his son holding a palette and brushes and wearing a fashionable ruff typical of contemporary aristo-cratic garb (fig. 20). The portrait has been interpreted as a statement concerning the artist's position in Spanish society as the equal of poets,

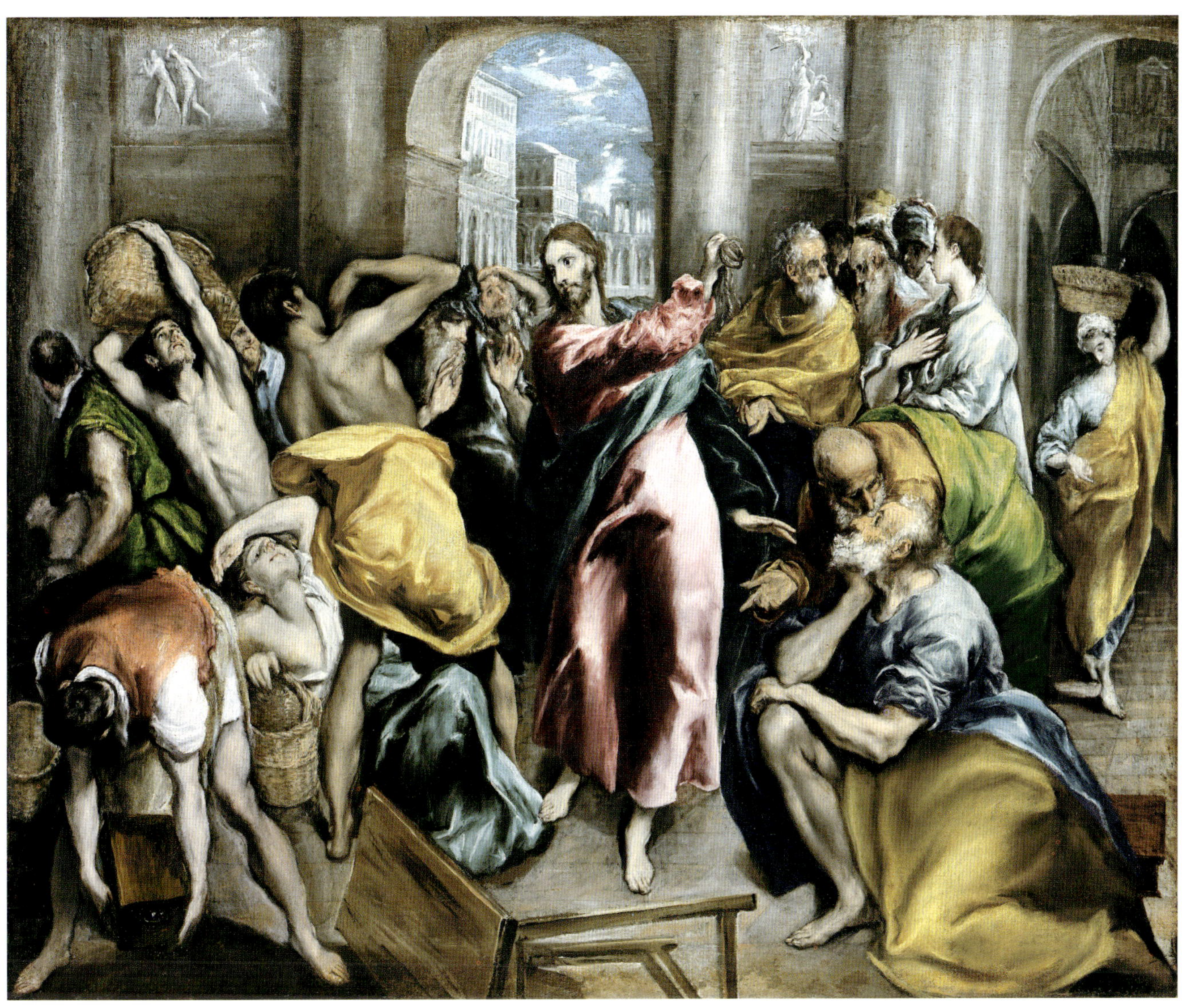

philosophers and rhetoricians rather than that of a mere craftsman. Jorge Manuel is shown holding his brush as a writer might hold his pen, a tool for communicating higher ideals.

One person who fully recognised El Greco's creative powers was the Trinitarian friar Hortensio Félix Paravicino y Arteaga (1580–1633), whose portrait El Greco painted around 1609 (fig. 21). The friar is shown wearing his black and white habit, sitting in a high-backed chair holding two books as though interrupting his studies to look up at us. A youthful prodigy, Paravicino was professor of rhetoric at the University of Salamanca by the age of twenty-one. He was a close friend of the poet Luís de Góngora and like him a practitioner of the rhetorical technique known as the *culterano* style. In this portrait, as in other late works, El Greco takes advantage of the reddish-brown ground painted over the

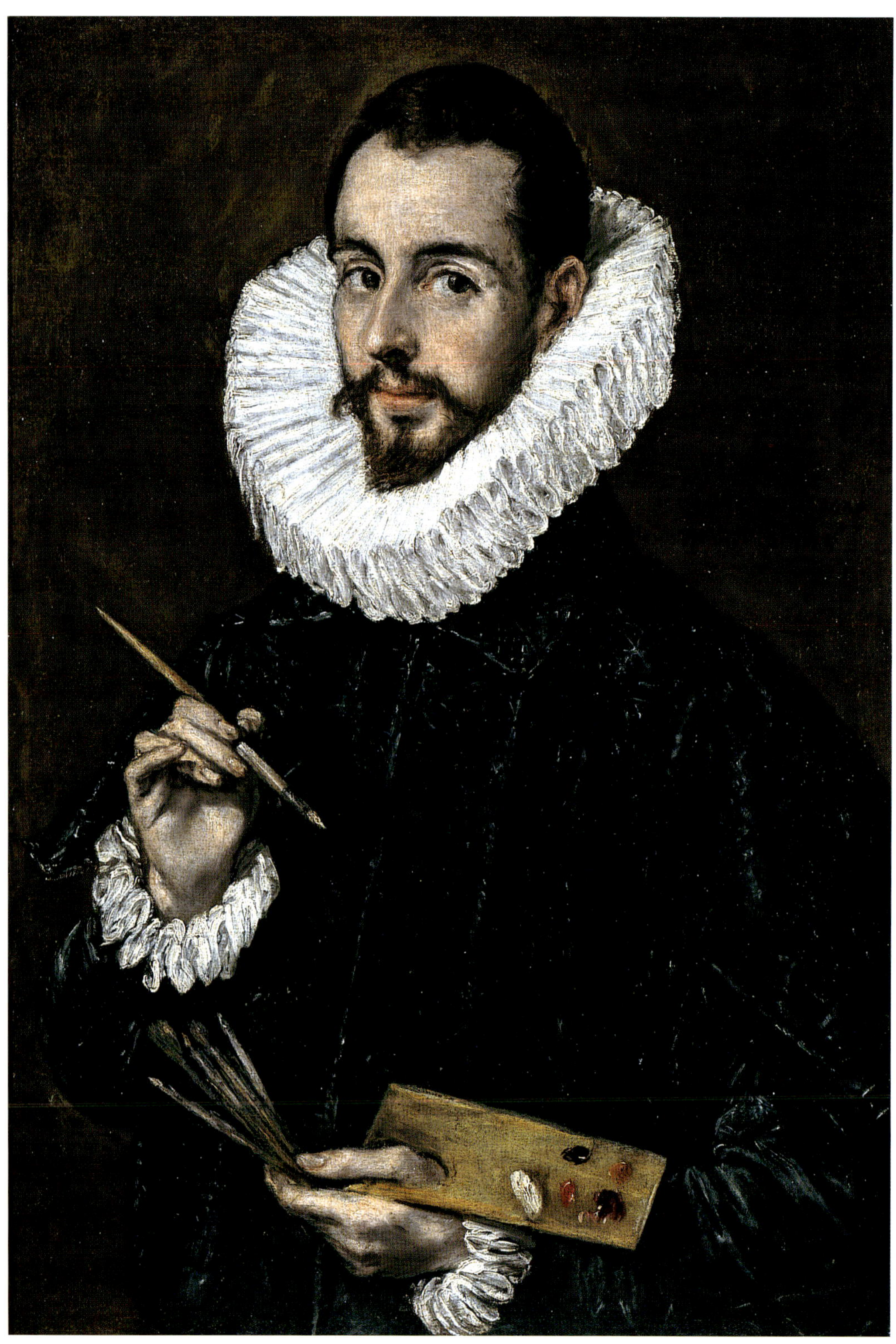

20. *An Artist (probably Jorge Manuel Theotokopoulos),* about 1600–5

Oil on canvas, 74 x 51.5 cm
Museo de Bellas Artes,
Seville

21. *Fray Hortensio Félix Paravicino,* about 1609

Oil on canvas, 112 x 86.1 cm
Museum of Fine Arts, Boston,
Isaac Sweetser Fund 1904, inv. 04.234

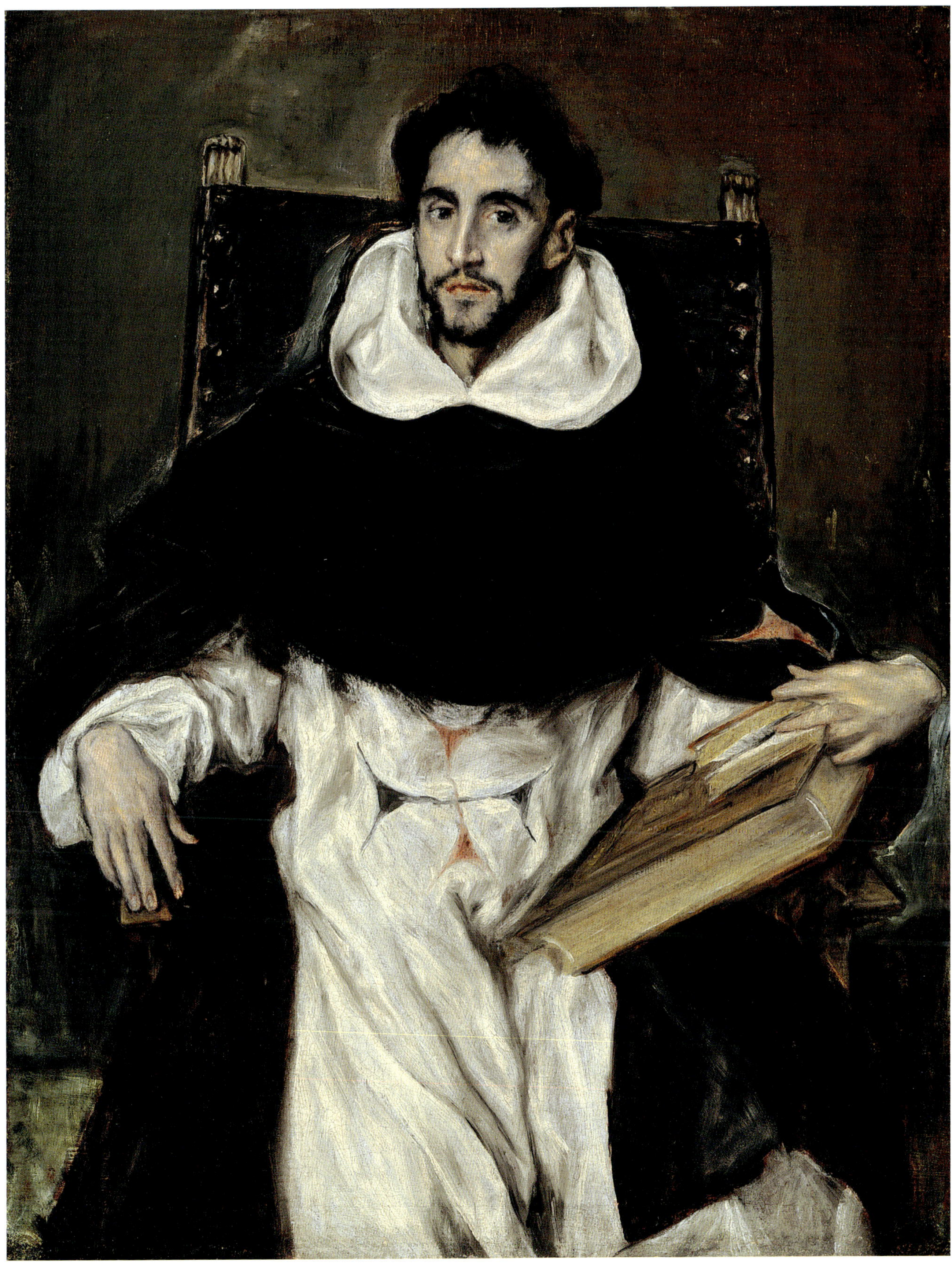

whole canvas as a key pictorial element, using it to define the shadowed areas of the white drapery and to give warmth to the background. The brushwork, free and spontaneous in all parts of the picture, enhances the vibrancy of the image, and the contrasting diagonals of the composition add a sense of vigour. From afar, the picture seems to blur the boundaries between reality and artifice to the point where Paravicino felt justified in suggesting in a sonnet dedicated to El Greco that his soul was at a loss to choose between his real body and his painted semblance. El Greco's approach to portraiture was to have a profound influence on Velázquez, who admired his works in the royal collection.

If an artist's ability to grasp and transmit a sense of beauty and grace – rather than literally to copy nature – constituted the glory of painting, a work that demonstrates El Greco's skills is *The Virgin of the Immaculate Conception* (fig. 22), executed between 1608 and 1613 for the Oballe Chapel in the Church of San Vicente in Toledo. At the bottom of the composition, El Greco has painted lilies and roses, the flowers of the Virgin, in a more realistic fashion than the figures above, so that as the viewer looks up he leaves the world of the senses and enters the visionary world of the spirit. In the upper half of the composition, the elongated figure of the Virgin in a blue cloak is being drawn up into heaven to be met by the Holy Spirit in the form of a dove. In the background, El Greco has painted a bird's-eye view of the city of Toledo. Ordered scale and proportion and anatomical accuracy have been subordinated to the imperatives of a visionary experience.

Although the interplay between the real world and the spiritual world was one of his principal philosophical concerns, El Greco's investigations into the relationship between sculpture and painting formed another fundamental aspect of his work. An inventory of his possessions made on his death in 1614 lists around thirty clay and wax models that he made, almost certainly as visual aids for painting his figures. One often sees the same figures, particularly of angels, painted from different angles in El Greco's work. He may have learnt this tech-nique from the Venetian painter Tintoretto, during his years in Venice. He would, however, have become especially aware of the relationship between sculpture and painting in the work of Michelangelo, particularly in the way the sculpted figure is re-used in a two-dimensional format. One of El Greco's surviving sculptures is a beautifully modelled and painted nude figure of *The Risen Christ* executed for the tabernacle of the main altar of the Tavera Hospital in 1595 (fig. 23). He re-used the same pose for his painted version of *The*

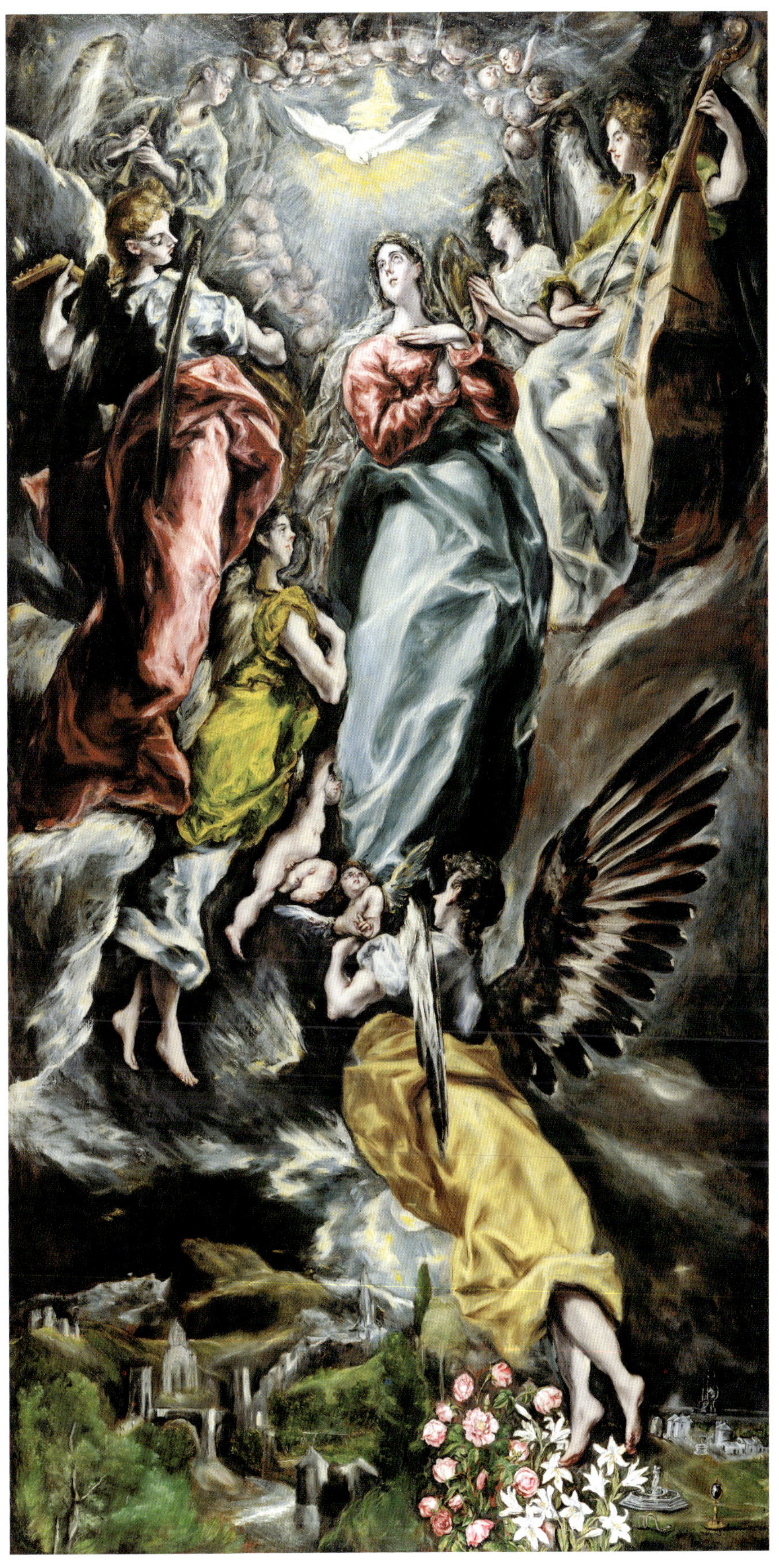

22. *The Virgin of the Immaculate Conception*
between 1608 and 1613

Oil on canvas, 348 x 174.5 cm
Parish of San Nicolás de Bari, Toledo,
now stored in the Museo de Santa Cruz,
Toledo, inv. 1277

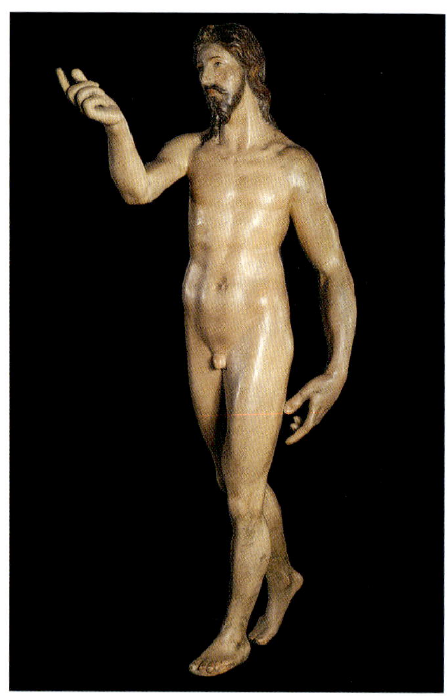

Resurrection (Museo Nacional del Prado, Madrid), proof that he worked with real form and then imbued it with a heightened sense of mysticism in his painting.

By the time that he had completed his painting for the Oballe Chapel, El Greco was in his late sixties or early seventies and had already enjoyed a much longer and richer life than many of his contemporaries. In 1612, he bought a burial space in the convent of Santo Domingo el Antiguo, where thirty-five years earlier he had painted one of his first commissions in Toledo and where his friends Diego and Luis de Castilla were interred. To decorate the altar above his own tomb, El Greco painted an *Adoration of the Shepherds* (fig. 24), in which the Christ Child lights up the composition with flame-like splendour. El Greco may have portrayed himself as one of the shepherds, possibly in the foreground kneeling in a gesture suggesting eternal supplication. He died soon after the painting was completed, on 7 April 1614. In his memory, Paravicino composed a funeral lament, a passage from which sums up El Greco's life:

> *Crete gave him life, Toledo his brushes*
> *And a better homeland, where through*
> *Death he began to achieve eternal life.*

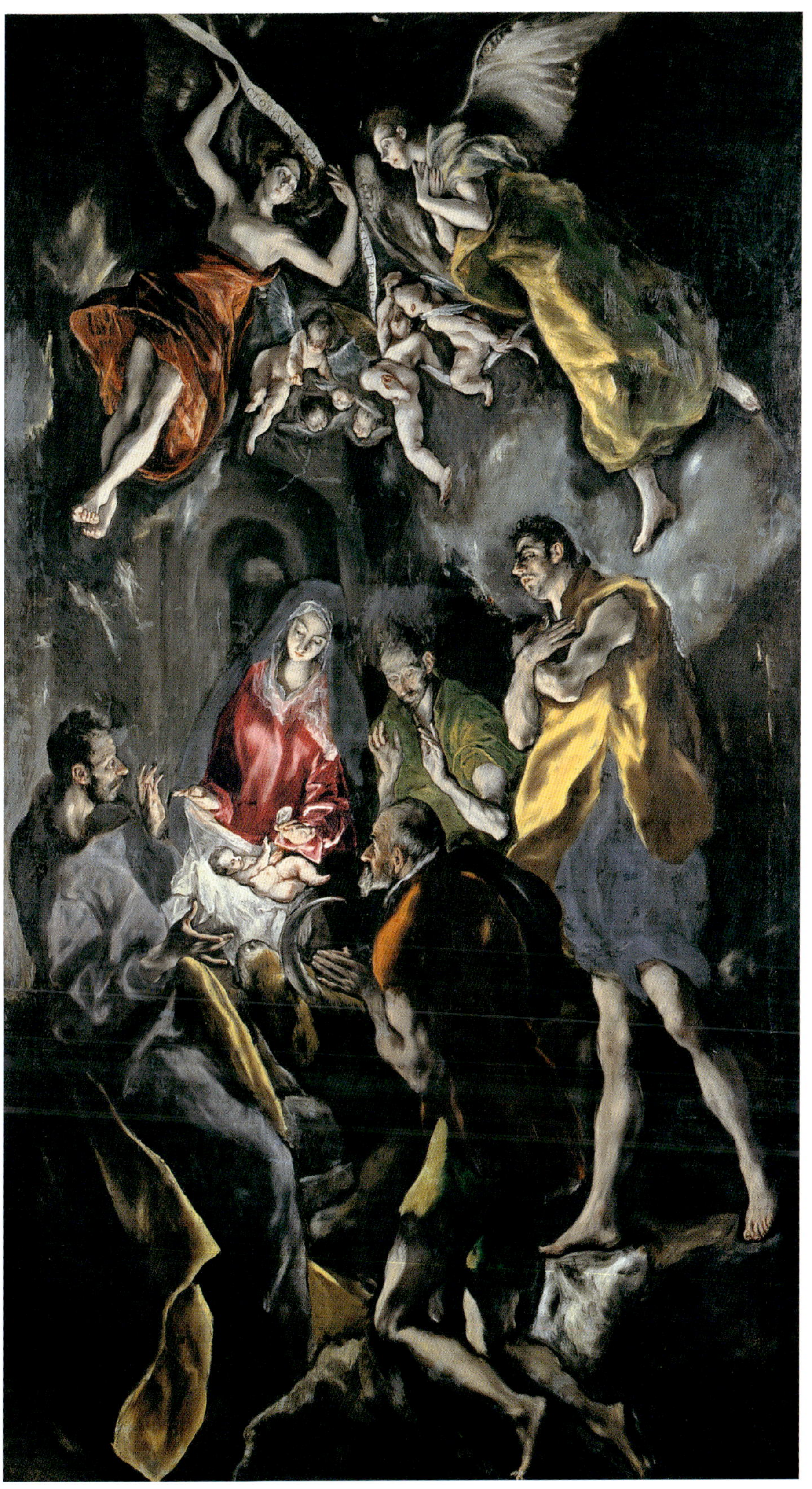

24. *The Adoration of the Shepherds*
about 1612–14

Oil on canvas, 319 x 180 cm
Museo Nacional del Prado, Madrid
inv. 2988

After El Greco's death, Jorge Manuel continued for a time to produce works based on his father's output. But fashions changed, and both El Greco and his son were soon forgotten as their visionary compositions gave way to Caravaggio's intense realism and different approaches to art and theology. Not until the nineteenth century did artists and critics such as the French painter Eugène Delacroix, the French critic and writer Théophile Gautier, and the Scottish art historian and traveller Sir William Stirling-Maxwell look once again, with any degree of attention, at El Greco's work. They found in him a highly individual manner of expression, summed up by Gautier in his *Voyage en Espagne* of 1845: 'There are abuses of light and dark, of violent contrasts, of singular colours, extravagant attitudes, draperies are shattered and crumpled haphazardly; but in all that there presides a depraved energy, an unhealthy strength that betrays the great painter and the madness of Genius.'

In the twentieth century, artists such as Franz Marc, Picasso and Jackson Pollock were among those who studied and admired El Greco's painting. In the *Blue Rider Almanac* of 1912, Franz Marc claimed that: 'Cézanne and El Greco are spiritual brothers, despite the centuries that separate them ... In their views of life both felt the mystical inner construction, which is the problem for our generation.' Picasso, meanwhile, asserted in relation to the origins of Cubism that 'we should look for Spanish influence in Cézanne ... Observe El Greco's influence on him. A Venetian painter, but he is Cubist in construction.'

One of El Greco's pictures that Picasso knew well was his unfinished *The Opening of the Fifth Seal* (fig. 25), which El Greco painted for the Tavera Hospital at the end of his life and which Picasso would have seen in the Parisian studio of the Basque painter Ignacio Zuloaga. Its visionary treatment of space and dematerialisation of form influenced Picasso in the genesis of his *Les Demoiselles d'Avignon* (Museum of Modern Art, New York). The film director Sergei Eisenstein, meanwhile, saw El Greco as one of the 'forefathers of film montage ... a forerunner of the newsreel' in the way he was able to edit his compositions to his liking, rejecting rules of perspective to obtain maximum effect.

El Greco, however, continued to confuse the general public. The British painter Paul Nash (1889–1946) recorded an amusing and yet revealing reaction to El Greco's *Laocoön* when it was lent to the National Gallery in London in 1934 by its then owner, the King of Yugoslavia. According to his review in *The Listener* magazine, the picture hung

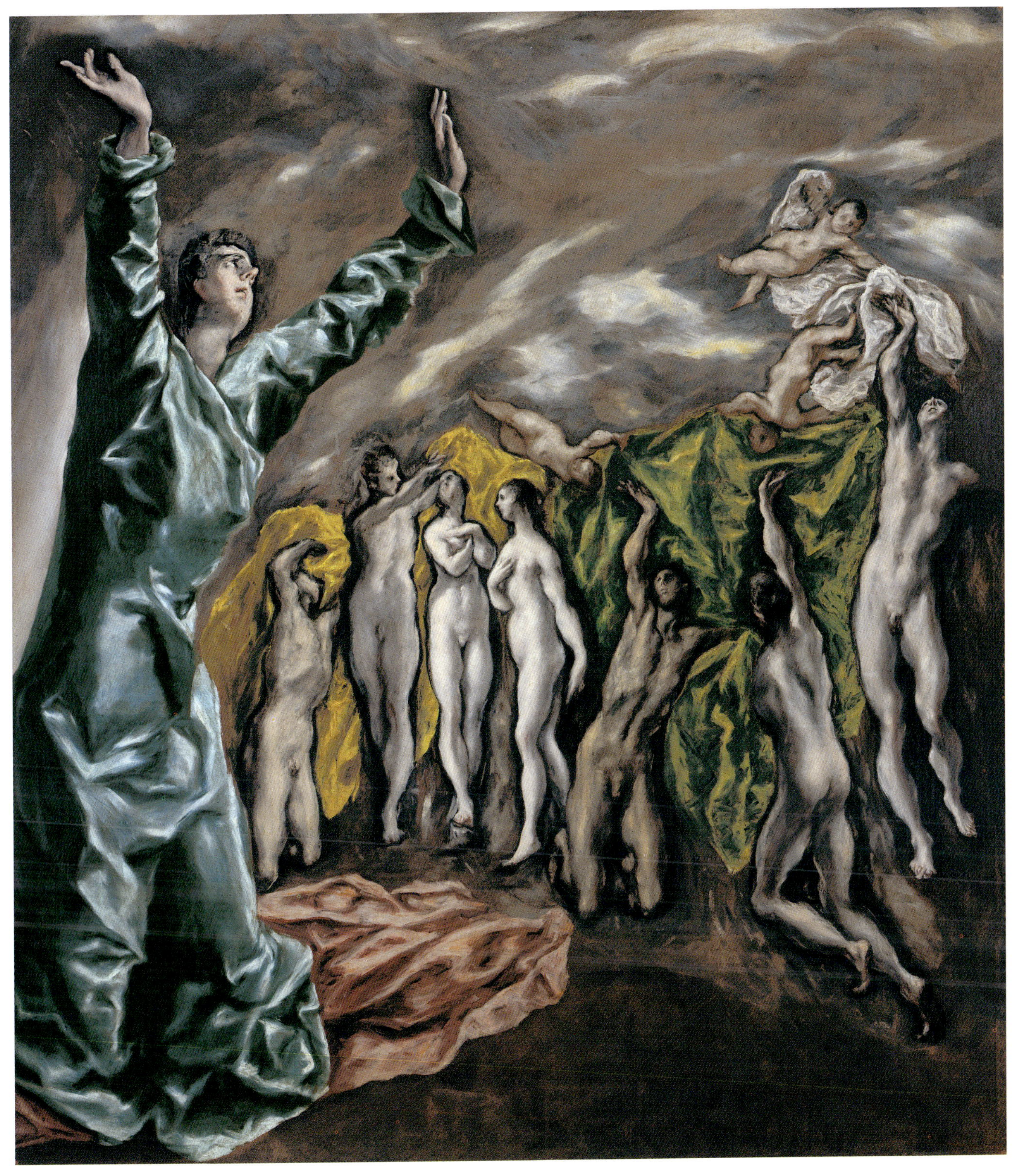

25. *The Opening of the Fifth Seal (The Vision of Saint John)*, 1608–14

Oil on canvas, 222.3 x 193 cm
The Metropolitan Museum of Art, New York
Rogers Fund, 1956, inv. 56.48

alongside three El Greco paintings owned by the National Gallery, *The Purification of the Temple*, *The Adoration of the Name of Jesus* and *The Agony in the Garden of Gethsemane*, with a Cézanne nearby to make the point of El Greco's modernity. Nash recorded the conversation of a confused couple of visitors:

Young Woman: *'What's that?'*
Young Man: *'It's by El Greco. He was a madman.'*
Young Woman: *'But would he be here – in the National Gallery?'*
Young Man: *'Oh, yes. There's another over on the other side, Cizzan, or something – a "Modern". All these "moderns" are mad; I read it in the Morning Post …'*

To understand El Greco's œuvre, one should remember his origins and the religious, philosophical, political and social contexts in which he worked. Only then can one begin to appreciate the function of his paintings and their significance for his audience. In Toledo, far from his birthplace, he fashioned an original response to the challenge of expressing the essence of religious dogma. His love of the arts, of literature and of philosophy, and the combined influences of his Cretan roots and his adopted Spanish home made him one of the most sophisticated artists of his time. Once the meaning of his mystical imagery becomes as clear for a modern viewer as it was for his patrons, many of the previously puzzling aspects of his painting fall into place. His way of looking at and interpreting his surroundings and the themes that he chose to depict in his paintings was to have no equal. Paravicino was not mistaken when he stated that 'Future ages will admire his genius, but none will imitate it'.

To my grandfather, Anthony Markham Bray, priest and scholar.

Brown, J., (ed.), *El Greco of Toledo*, exh. cat., Museo del Prado, Madrid; National Gallery of Art, Washington; The Toledo Museum of Art, Toledo (Ohio); Dallas Museum of Fine Art, Dallas, 1982–3

Davies, D., *El Greco*, Oxford and London 1976

Davies, D., (ed.), *El Greco*, exh. cat., The Metropolitan Museum of Art, New York; The National Gallery, London, 2003

Mann, R.G., *El Greco and His Patrons. Three major projects*, Cambridge 1986

Wethey, H.E., *El Greco and his School*, 2 vols, Princeton 1962

CHRONOLOGY

CRETE

1541 Domenikos Theotokopoulos, (known as El Greco) is born in Candia (now Iraklion), the capital of Crete. He trains as an icon painter on the island and by his early twenties is a master painter.

1566 *26 December* El Greco sells a *Passion of Christ* (now lost) by lottery.

1567 El Greco probably leaves Crete for Venice during the spring or summer.

ITALY

1568 *August* El Greco is recorded living in Venice, where he is greatly influenced by the work of Titian and Tintoretto.

1570 El Greco travels to Rome and finds lodgings in the Farnese palace, on the recommendation of the artist Giulio Clovio. There he mixes with an elite circle of intellectuals, including the Farnese librarian Fulvio Orsini (see p. 14) and Luis de Castilla, son of the dean of Toledo cathedral, who later becomes an important contact in Spain.

1571 *7 October* The Ottoman Turks are defeated at the Battle of Lepanto by the Holy League. El Greco later paints an allegory of this alliance (see fig. 9).

1572 *6 July* For unknown reasons El Greco is ejected from the Farnese Palace.

18 September El Greco registers with the artists' guild under the name 'Dominico Greco', the first record of him using this name.

SPAIN

1576 *21 October* El Greco appeals for financial aid from the Royal Almoner in Madrid.

1577 *July 1* El Greco receives an advance payment for *The Disrobing of Christ* for Toledo Cathedral (fig. 11), commissioned through Diego de Castilla, dean of Toledo Cathedral.

8 August El Greco is commissioned by Diego de Castilla to provide three altarpieces for the new Church of Santo Domingo el Antiguo (fig. 12).

1578 El Greco's son, Jorge Manuel, is born (see fig. 20).

1579 The paintings for Santo Domingo el Antiguo are completed. The valuation of *The Disrobing of Christ* for Toledo cathedral on 15 June leads to the first of a series of legal disputes that become a feature of almost all of El Greco's important commissions.

1581 The dispute, over both the price of and iconography within *The Disrobing of Christ* is finally resolved.

1582 *16 November* El Greco delivers *The Martyrdom of Saint Maurice* (fig. 10) to El Escorial, but Philip II dislikes it and orders a replacement from another painter. This ends El Greco's hopes of a court appointment.

1585 *10 September* El Greco rents rooms in the palace of the Marqués de Villena. He continues to live there until at least 1590.

1586 *18 March* El Greco is commissioned to paint *The Burial of the Count of Orgaz* (fig. 13) for the Parish Church of Santo Tomé.

1596 *17 December* El Greco is commissioned to provide an altarpiece for the Church of the Augustine College of Doña María de Aragón, Madrid.

1597 *9 November* El Greco signs a contract with Dr Martín Ramírez de Zayas, professor of theology at the University of Toledo, to paint three altarpieces for his private family chapel of Saint Joseph, Toledo (figs 15 and 16).

1598 Philip II dies and his son Philip III is proclaimed King of Spain.

1599 *13 December* The paintings for the Chapel of Saint Joseph are valued. After an initial challenge, Zayas agrees to pay the full price of 2850 ducats.

1600 *12 July* The paintings for the college of Doña María de Aragón are delivered. Despite difficulties obtaining payment, El Greco eventually receives nearly 6000 ducats for his work.

1603 From this year Jorge Manuel appears in documents as his father's assistant and business partner. On 18 June, 'Domingo Greco and Xorhe Manuel, painters' receive a commission for an altarpiece for the Hospital de la Caridad, Illescas.

1604 *5 August* El Greco returns to live in the palace of the Marqués de Villena. He remains there for the rest of his life.

1604 *13 December* Manuel Griego (probably the artist's brother, Manoussos Theotokopoulos), is recorded in the book of the deceased in El Greco's Parish Church of Santo Tomé.

1605 *4 August* The work at Illescas is completed. The price is the subject of a bitter and lengthy litigation, which is only finally resolved in 1607.

1607 *11 December* El Greco is commissioned to provide an altarpiece for the Oballe Chapel, Toledo (fig. 22).

1608 *16 November* El Greco receives his last large commission for three altars in the Chapel of the Tavera Hospital, Toledo (fig. 25).

1611 *12 August* Having fallen two years behind in their rent, El Greco and and Jorge Manuel have to negotiate a back payment with the agents of the Marqués de Villena.

1611 *19 November* Following the death of Philip II's widow, Margarita of Austria, the councillors of Toledo commission El Greco and Jorge Manuel to provide a monument for funerary celebrations in Toledo Cathedral; the monument is praised in a sonnet by Hortensio Félix Paravicino, whose portrait El Greco had painted a couple of years earlier (fig. 21).

1612 *26 August* El Greco purchases a family burial vault in the Church of Santo Domingo el Antiguo, Toledo; in payment he agrees to build the altar and retable at his own expense. It is for this chapel that he paints *The Adoration of the Shepherds* (fig. 24).

1614 *7 April* El Greco dies and is buried at Santo Domingo el Antiguo. Jorge Manuel draws up an inventory of his possessions and completes many of the paintings left unfinished in El Greco's studio, continuing his father's business until his own death in 1631.

This book was published to accompany the exhibition *El Greco* at the National Gallery, London 11 February – 23 May 2004. Exhibition supported by

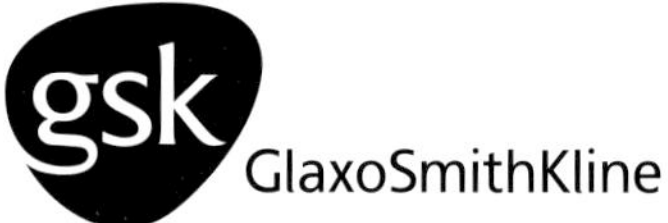

© 2004 National Gallery Company Limited
Reprinted 2004

First published in Great Britain in 2004 by
National Gallery Company Limited
St Vincent House, 30 Orange Street, London WC2H 7HH
www.nationalgallery.co.uk

ISBN 1 85709 315 1
525473

British Library Cataloguing-in-Publication Data
A catalogue record is available from the British Library
Library of Congress Catalog Card Number 200302051

Publisher Kate Bell
Editor Jane Ace
Designer Peter Campbell
Picture Researcher Xenia Corcoran
Production Jane Hyne and Penny Le Tissier

Printed and bound in Italy by Conti Tipocolor

Front Cover: Detail of *A View of Toledo*, about 1597–9 (fig. 14)
Back Cover: *Saint Luke painting the Virgin and Child*, before 1567 (fig. 3)
Frontispiece: Detail of *The Virgin of the Immaculate Conception*, between 1608 and 1613 (fig. 22)

All measurements give height before width